Wasted

COUNTING THE COSTS OF

GLOBAL CONSUMPTION

A European city with one million inhabitants requires on average more than 10,000 (metric) tons of fossil fuels, more than 300,000 tons of water and 2,000 tons of food per day, and at the same time it produces 1,500 tons of harmful emissions, 300,000 tons of waste-water and 1,600 tons of solid waste.

Dr Klaus Topfer,
German Minister for Regional Planning, in
UNED-UK 1995 (p5)

The concept of sustainable development recognises that both economic and environmental factors affect the quality of life and must be taken into account in decision-making. This means that the full environmental costs – as well as the economic cost – should, as far as possible, be taken into account in any new development. That includes taking account of the environmental impact of the waste that is likely to arise from any product or person.

Department of the Environment 1995 (p2)

Yet as soon as we admit that dealing with environmental problems may entail cuts in standards of living, the question of who will pay becomes central; the more significant the costs, the greater the potential distributional conflicts.

Bhaskar and Glyn 1995 (p3)

In an empty world economy, [the commodity and its price] could be regarded as the only material consequences of relevance, since the other material consequences of the productive activity, such as waste, would have no effect on human welfare if they simply disappeared through ecosystem recycling and dissipation. In a full world, on the other hand, this is no longer true. These other material consequences do not disappear: consumers are 'buying' a whole package of material consequences along with the commodity.

Barth 1996 (pp23–24)

MICHAEL REDCLIFT

Wasted

COUNTING THE COSTS OF
GLOBAL CONSUMPTION

EARTHSCAN

Earthscan Publications Ltd, London

http://www.earthscan.co.uk

First published in the UK in 1996 by
Earthscan Publications Limited

A catalogue record for this book is available from the British Library

ISBN 1 85383 355 X (Paperback)
ISBN 1 85383 360 6 (Hardback)

Typesetting by JS Typesetting, Wellingborough, Northants.
Printed and bound by Biddles Ltd, Guildford and King's Lynn.
Cover design by Andrew Corbett

For a full list of publications please contact:

Earthscan Publications Limited
120 Pentonville Road
London N1 9JN
Tel: 0171 278 0433
Fax: 0171 278 1142
Email: earthsales@earthscan.co.uk

Earthscan is an editorially independent subsidiary of Kogan Page Limited
and publishes in association with WWF-UK and the International Institute
for Environment and Development.

To Becky and Victoria

Contents

Acknowledgments   xi
List of Figures   xii
List of Tables   xiii

Chapter One   Introduction   1
  Consumption and the environment   5
  How can we 'recover consumption'?   8

Chapter Two   The Earth Summit   11
  International environmental policy: the road from
  Stockholm   12
  Counsel of despair: international environmental problems
  in the 1980s   15
  UNCED: the road to Rio   19
  The UNCED deliberations: conventions and a new agenda   23
  In the wake of Rio: international finance and political
  devolution   28
  Global environmental management: a realist perspective   31
  From science to policy: environmental management and
  the UNCED process   34
  Making sense of the environment/development debate   36

Chapter Three   Meeting Environmental Targets   **39**
   Global environmental change   40
   The laws of thermodynamics   42
   The effect of human evolution on natural systems   44
   Sustainable development   47
   Sustainability indicators   49

Chapter Four   The Global Economy and Consumption   **61**
   The hydrocarbon society and energy consumption   62
   The new international economic order   72
   Energy consumption and the generation of waste   79
   Recovering consumption: the political economy of wastes   82

Chapter Five   Managing Global Resources   **91**
   European energy policy and global change   92
   Sustainable energy policies for the Brazilian Amazon   100

Chapter Six   Metabolising Nature   **109**
   Global environmental management   110
   The 'empty' and 'full' world system: a point of departure   111
   How we measure environmental quality: the costs of
   consumption   114
   Democratic control of the environment   117
   The standard of living or the quality of life?   119
   Global carbon budgets   123
   The social functions of sinks   129

Chapter Seven   Sustainability and Social Commitments   133
   Environmental discourse and environmental management   136
   How we metabolise nature   141
   Embodiment and distanciation   144

Chapter Eight   Local Environmental Action   **149**
   Creating sustainable employment: LETS schemes   151
   Beyond recycling: recovering our control over waste   153
   Farmers' networks   156

References   161

Index   169

Acknowledgments

Earlier drafts of this book were written while I was Director of the ESRC's Global Environmental Change Programme. I would like to acknowledge the help of Alister Scott and Ann Wakefield, who worked with me on the GEC Programme, and of all the researchers under the Programme, from whom I learnt such a lot. Thanks also to David Cooper, for compiling the index. Any errors of judgement or fact are, of course, solely mine.

List of Figures

4.1   Energy consumption per person, selected countries,
       1992   63
4.2   World primary energy consumption, 1850–1980   64
4.3   Primary energy consumption relative to real GDP,
       selected countries, 1850–1982   65
4.4   Total commercial energy consumption by region,
       1970–1990   66
4.5   Total commercial energy consumption by source,
       1970–1990   66
4.6   Commodity structure of world trade, 1965 and 1986   69
4.7   Global income and economic disparities   73
4.8   Where people will be in 2025   75
4.9   The world's 15 largest economies, 1992 and 2020   77
4.10 China's electricity generation capacity, 1981–2000   79
4.11 Numbers of automobiles worldwide, 1950–1990   85
4.12 GDP and output of pollutants in Indonesia, The
       Philippines and Thailand, 1975–1988   87
4.13 Major international transfers of hazardous wastes   89
5.1   The location of hydropower plants in the Amazon   102
6.1   The finite global ecosystem relative to the growing
       economic subsystem   112
6.2   Comparative values of greenhouse gas emissions of
       WRI's top ten emitting nations   125
7.1   A model of human use of the environment   134
7.2   The universe of the undiscussed   146

List of Tables

4.1   Population growth and energy consumption, 1960–1984   71
4.2   Real GDP growth, North and South, annual average   74
4.3   Growth rates of world electricity consumption,
       1971–1989   78
4.4   Quantities of municipal waste generated, by country,
       1980 and 1990   82
4.5   Waste disposal routes, by country   83
4.6   Urban densities and commuting choices in selected
       cities   84
5.1   Energy production in Europe, 1990   95
5.2   Energy demand in Europe, 1990   95
5.3   Carbon dioxide emissions, 1990 (United Kingdom)   99
5.4   Brazilian energy consumption, 1990–2020   101
6.1   Consumption classes: the global picture   120
6.2   Comparative resource consumption, North and South   121
6.3   How quickly must fossil fuels be phased out?   127

Chapter One

Introduction

This book was written from a sense of acute unease with the rhetoric that has accompanied 'sustainable development' since the report of the Brundtland Commission, *Our Common Future*, was published (WCED 1987). My unease was compounded by the events during and after the Earth Summit, which was held in Rio de Janeiro in 1992. This story has been told elsewhere (Chatterjee and Finger 1994). My purpose in this book is to examine the assumptions behind our understanding of 'sustainable development', and the idea that environmental management can, and should, be practised at a global level.

We cannot begin to 'manage' the environment successfully at the global level without first achieving progress towards sustainability at the local level. This we have signally failed to do, and yet we are seeking to construct an apparatus to deal with specifically 'global' problems, through institutions like the Global Environment Facility. We are, in effect, inventing new institutional structures for managing the environment, which bear little or no relation to the processes through which the environment is transformed. There is little correspondence between the processes that drive unsustainable development, and the management tools and political institutions which are supposed to achieve greater global sustainability.

It is the contention of this book that sustainable development is a normative goal for societies, one that is imbued with values, and

1

frequently implies value judgements. It is also a concept or model for understanding ecosystems. As a social goal sustainability is bound up with everyday practices, and familiar social institutions. To achieve sustainable development we should look no further than our own behaviour, and the economic and social institutions we have constructed which need to be radically overhauled. We are accustomed to speak about bequeathing the environment to future generations, but frequently baulk at the idea that we are also bequeathing social institutions with which to manage the environment. Sustainability will not be achieved by inventing management techniques to combat the contradictions of development. *It can only be achieved by incorporating a knowledge of the consequences of our behaviour into the behaviour itself.* This book outlines the importance of this objective, and its implications, particularly for those of us in the industrialised world. To achieve sustainability we need to recover our control over consumption, rather than invent new institutions to manage its consequences.

To some extent my position owes much to those who have already identified the deficiencies of both our economic policies, and the models which we use to interpret them. Foremost among these is Herman Daly, and his advocacy of 'steady-state' economics, as an antidote to 'growthmania'. Daly writes:

> The economy grows in physical scale, but the ecosystem does not. Therefore, as the economy grows it becomes larger in relation to the ecosystem. Standard economics does not ask how large the economy should be relative to the ecosystem.
>
> (Daly 1987, 180)

Herman Daly's insight is discussed further in Chapter Six below. My intention in this book, however, is to take the discussion beyond the environment and economic theory, and to address the social processes which underpin our economic behaviour, and the structure of global political economy which makes the achievement of sustainable development so difficult.

At the heart of the matter lies the question of consumption. In a highly provocative paper about sustainability, Robert Goodland, an economist with the World Bank, makes a very challenging assertion. He argues that raising *per capita* incomes in poor countries to between $1500 and $2000 is quite possible. If this were to be done then people living at this level of consumption would benefit from 80 per cent of the basic welfare provided by incomes ten times as high in the North (c$15,000–$20,000). He adds:

> [those] working on Northern *overconsumption* should address the corollary – can $21,000 *per capita* countries (OECD) *cut their consumption* by a factor of ten, and suffer 'only' a 20 per cent loss of basic welfare?
>
> (Goodland 1994, 8)

In the context of continuing economic growth we surely need to ask some leading questions: how much more welfare does additional material consumption actually buy? What would be the environmental and social benefits of reducing our consumption to more modest proportions? Could we design an alternative vision which enabled progress to be made in improving human welfare, without damaging the environment, and without significant welfare costs for most people in the North?

The urgency of these questions, as discussed in Chapter Three, is underlined by the growth of emulative consumption in much of the South, particularly the fast-growing economies of Asia. In the South, television ownership increased by 400 per cent between 1975 and 1989. In India there is evidence of more 'television-friendly' foods being consumed. For example, wheat-based chappatis are less often served on Sunday evenings when the evening movies are screened. And, of course, the images and advertising that fill the television screens (from STAR and ARABSAT and CNN) are of developed-country consumption. (The environments that are captured on television screens, North and South, as a part of the global tourist industry, are often – significantly – those of the South).

The problem with the 'development' agenda, then, is that in the real world meeting economic and social targets is impossible without raising consumption, both the volume and the kinds of goods we produce. Given the absolute limits on our natural resources, and the fact that our 'development' is placing more emphasis on the 'sink' functions of our natural forests and grasslands, we are clearly increasing the vulnerability of natural resource systems. As Wolfgang Sachs has put it, our

> unfettered enthusiasm for economic growth in 1945 reflected the West's desire to restart the economic machine after a devastating war.
>
> (Sachs 1991, 252)

We have still not outgrown this preoccupation.

However, faced with the difficulties, constraints and contradictions of 'development', we have begun to cast the argument for growth differently, relying on the qualifying adjective, 'sustainable', and the idea of development, to help ourselves out of the impasse. Environment and development is indeed, as Sachs suggests, the story of a dangerous liaison . . .

Is there an alternative to unsustainable development, besides grandiose, and unworkable, schemes for global management? I think there is, and want to argue that it begins with redefining the problem, following Daly, around ways of making consumption more sustainable. 'Recovering' consumption means both reducing existing waste and producing less waste in future. It also means conserving sinks, not merely because forests and water sources contain valuable species, but because without them we cannot consume at all. It means, to coin a phrase from the current policy discourse in Britain, replacing 'technology foresight' (increasing the United Kingdom's competitiveness in international markets) with 'environmental foresight' (ensuring that we add to, rather than detract from, the accumulative value of natural capital stock).

As we shall see, increasing the lifespan of goods and services, and reducing adverse environmental impacts, also carries implications for our attitudes to consumption itself, and to such modern cultural icons as fashion, disposability and novelty. Although this book does not attempt it, any comprehensive treatment of modern consumption needs to grapple with its cultural concomitants: why do we *need* to consume? As the cultural historians John Brewer and Roy Porter make clear, material culture in the seventeenth and eighteenth centuries provides illuminating insights into society itself (Brewer and Porter 1993). There is every bit as much to be gained from examining the material culture of our own period, for insights into the preferences and prejudices of our own societies.

This book is also concerned to build bridges between sociological analysis, and the analysis of the underlying social commitments which define consumption, and global political economy. This is because, in my judgement, we need both. We need to understand why our commitments, and practices, carry implications for the environment that are difficult (although not impossible) to change. We also need to examine the economic structures, particularly those linking the developed and developing countries, which serve to maintain patterns of consumption and to ignore the consequences. It is important, if we are to explain the links between physical processes and social behaviour, to understand the logic of market capitalism, and the forces that drive the world economic system.

Much of the argument about deregulation today, and increasingly 're-regulation' around the environment, is conducted as if there were no issues surrounding the economic ideology and structures which caused the problems in the first place.

CONSUMPTION AND THE ENVIRONMENT

The study of consumption has a long and distinguished pedigree, encompassing a number of disciplines, among which perhaps history and anthropology are the most notable. As Brewer and Porter comment, historians have, for the most part, regarded the 'world of goods' in a relatively unsystematic way, rarely bringing the insights of cultural, economic and political historians together (Brewer and Porter 1993). A number of useful, and occasionally brilliant, studies exist of individual commodities and goods but few studies of the history of consumer societies. Pioneering work, like that of Veblen, has failed to galvanise the interest of the social sciences during most of the twentieth century (Veblen 1899).

In the United Kingdom the analysis of 'goods and things', as the historian Asa Briggs described them, has frequently led to useful insights about the society from which they sprang (Briggs 1988). Some studies have shown how the development of class taste, and its manifestation in increasing consumption, is closely linked to economic expansion at the level of cities and the nation state. The Edwardian house, to give but one illustration, provides a window onto the fortunes of whole classes, involved in its construction, furnishing and occupation (Long 1993).

In particular, little attention has been given, until recently, to the way in which our consumption influences our environmental perceptions and values. Even our food preferences are rarely associated with transformations in the 'natural' environment (Goodman and Redclift 1991).

Another increasingly important contribution to the discussion of consumption, is that of anthropology (Miller 1987, Miller 1995). Anthropologists have always been interested in 'goods', in terms of exchange and value, taking their cue from Marcel Mauss' classic study (Mauss 1954). The study of mass consumption, and of ideas about objectification and material culture, has emerged, together with 'cultural studies', as an important area for analysts of contemporary culture (Lee 1993). Baudrillard, among others, presents an account of the way in which commodities are interchanged, which reduces human relations to questions of style (Baudrillard 1981). However, as Campbell comments, the theorists within the social sciences who are usually quoted in connection with consumption (Walter Benjamin, Erving Goffman, Henri Lefebvre) are more properly theorists of culture, or of post-modernity, rather than theorists of consumption. (Campbell 1995).

More recent post-modern theory has given considerable attention to consumption. One example is Lash, who draws our attention to the differences between the semiotics of consumption, the 'sign values' communicated by style, taste and fashion, and the kind of objective limits to consumption which are established by markets. What Lash calls the 'coherent limits to the level of human demands' constitute the principal focus of this book, and it is a focus which has been largely ignored by post-modernism (Lash 1990,40). Partial exceptions are the recent interest not only in the symbolic importance of landscape, tourism and leisure, but the sense of 'place' which this engenders (Bird, Curtis, Putnam, Robertson and Tickner 1993, Urry 1995).

Without wishing to minimise the importance of consumption to societies in the wider sense, the argument of this book is about the material parameters within which consumption occurs. It is not principally concerned with globalisation as a cultural process (Featherstone 1990) although, as Barth argues, 'the two ranges of issues become so closely interconnected that they will need to be addressed within some kind of encompassing perspective' (Barth 1996, 21). The principal focus is the material consequences of the way that the environment is constructed socially, a construction which is increasingly global in reach. It is argued that we need to begin to assume responsibility for the material consequences of our actions, the effects of enhanced consumption on the environment and social welfare, before we can make any real inroads into the log-jam of global agreements.

One point of departure is the concern which some Green thinkers, and many more environmental groups, have expressed with Northern 'overconsumption' during the last few decades. Recent studies have commented on the way in which those in (formal) employment seek to maximise their income, rather than their leisure, in order to consume more. This is what Schor has called the 'work and spend' cycle (Schor 1995). There is some evidence that people in the developed countries today are less likely than their parents or grandparents were to trade-off increased leisure time against working time. Similarly, those in formal employment are also likely to play a dominant role in informal or 'black economy' work (Pahl and Wallace 1985). There are a number of facets to this prioritisation of work, and consumption, over leisure. Schor adds:

> The existence of a work and spend cycle has a number of implications. First, it suggests an addictive aspect to consumption. Over time, people become habituated or "addicted" to the level of consumption which they are attaining. Goods which are originally experienced as luxuries come to be seen as necessities.
>
> (Schor 1995, 74)

The Role of NGOs

What can loosely be termed 'Green thinking' has often focused upon the importance of distinguishing between 'needs' and 'wants' (*Illich 1975, Schumacher 1973, Porritt 1984*). Essentially, needs require satisfaction, but the way that they are satisfied can vary widely, and consumer societies may successfully create new 'wants' without satisying even basic needs. The idea of a hierarchy of needs, first put forward by Maslow (1954), is often understood at an intuitive level by the population at large, and prompts the interest both in reducing waste (recycling and re-use) and in the vast expansion of voluntary-sector activities, on behalf of the homeless and others, which have helped to fill the gap left by the retreat of the state since the early 1980s. Non-governmental organisations (NGOs) such as Friends of the Earth, Greenpeace and Oxfam, have been at the forefront of demands to place Northern consumption within the context of North/South trade, global environmental destruction and the transport of wastes. Attention has been given to ways in which Northern consumers can make choices that are less prejudicial to the developing countries without ceasing to be 'global consumers' (Wells and Jetter 1991).

The presence of NGOs, and the pressure mounted by them, was a major factor in stimulating the events leading up to the Rio Summit in 1992, and since then it is largely the NGOs, increasingly in alliance, that have forced national governments to consider the relationship between levels of consumption, waste and the environment. At the same time it is important to separate NGO environmental campaigns in the North from grass-roots activities in the South. As Parnwell and Bryant (1996) point out, in South East Asia, NGOs have been unable to match global concern with reversals in official policy, despite unrelenting campaigns.

HOW CAN WE 'RECOVER CONSUMPTION'?

These issues of the relationship between the environment and consumption, and the impact on North/South relations, are taken up at different stages in this book. It is argued that we need to begin by examining the recent background to attempts at global environmental management, leading to the 1992 Earth Summit. At the same time the ability to meet international obligations is conditional; it depends critically on the growth in the global economy, and the relationships that are emerging between different parts of the global economic system. A political economy approach thus lies at the heart of the analysis.

At the same time any attempt to 'recover' our power over consumption necessitates a clear understanding of how and why we use natural resources in the way we do, how we 'metabolise' nature. In the latter part of this book, the process of metabolisation is linked to social values and behaviour, leading to an analysis of the underlying social commitments (our unexplored behaviour) which carries fundamental implications for the environment. The conclusion is that an analysis of global economic processes needs to be closely linked to social processes at a number of levels, including that of individuals and local communities. Ultimately, meeting environmental targets will become increasingly difficult, and the goalposts constantly change position, unless we can match our consumption of energy and goods to ecological trends in the real world. The implications of this approach are uncomfortable: both changes in global political economy and individual lifestyles are needed.

In Chapter Two of this book, *The Earth Summit*, the recent history of global environmental negotiations is discussed, in the context of the various forces and 'political blocs' which appeared at the Earth Summit in 1992, and which have led to frustrated attempts at global environmental management. The prospects of successfully refashioning global agreements are also explored. In Chapter Three (*Meeting Environmental Targets*), global environmental change is discussed as an historical process, beginning with the Industrial Revolution in Europe.

The chapter goes on to explore the relationship between human evolution and natural systems, and the way in which cultural evolution enabled human societies to distance themselves conceptually from their environments. It is argued that 'sustainable development' needs to be viewed from within this evolving process, as providing the normative framework for environmental management. The final section discusses sustainability indicators, arguing that achieving sustainability is not simply a question of establishing 'targets', but also of incorporating sustainability within political choices, making sustainability a central element in mainstream political discourse.

Chapter Four (*The Global Economy and Consumption*) focuses on the political economy of global environmental change. It begins by considering the evolution of a development model based on hydrocarbons, which have fuelled global consumption, and the environmental costs of this model. The impact of shifts in the Northern industrialised countries on the countries of the South is explored. The form of integration between the industrialised and less industrialised worlds, including the newly industrialising countries (NICs), guarantees a replication of the North's pattern of consumption, and the transfer of environmental problems associated with industrialised economies, although often in a form that carries critical environmental costs.

Chapter Five (*Managing Global Resources*) takes this argument to the level of global regions. Focusing on energy consumption, and taking the cases of Europe and Brazil, it is argued that the decisions dictating policies, and the way that environmental problems are understood, avoid serious consideration of sustainability. In Europe the issue is the convergence of energy policies, rather than their cumulative effect. In Brazil it is the way in which the development model, prompted by population increase, is laying waste the Amazon, a sink of last resort for global society.

Chapter Six (*Metabolising Nature*) suggests that if global environmental management is the goal of the new international discourse, we also need to ask why some environmental functions, such as that of carbon sinks, are regarded as 'natural' in the first place, and why we do not make conscious attempts to protect them for the environmental 'services' they perform. This leads to a consideration of what lies behind environmental management: the economic ideology and practices that serve to metabolise nature, and to transform resources, and environmental services, into the production of commodities.

Chapter Seven (*Sustainability and Social Commitments*) takes the argument into the cultural domain, considering the way in which our inattention to our underlying cultural practices, or social commitments, has driven patterns of consumption, and carries environmental costs that we fail to recognise. The argument develops from the earlier discussion of consumption and the environment, in that the forces driving consumption are looked upon as 'cultural' in a more inclusive sense. They lie in our conception of needs and wants, and the process through which links between developed and developing countries have appropriated the use of resources and sinks in the South. Our underlying social commitments have developed historically, together with increasingly globalised economic relations.

Finally, Chapter Eight (*Local Environmental Action*) considers the way in which local struggles to secure a livelihood – in the North as well as the South – are helping to define the global political agenda. The achievement of sustainability may be remote, and few people may be concerned with it as a goal, but the efforts to secure employment and to ensure personal security and welfare cannot be divorced from environmental considerations. This chapter takes three case studies, one in employment, another in waste management, the third in food policy to illustrate the connections between livelihoods, social welfare and environmental sustainability. It seeks to demonstrate that resistance to many aspects of globalisation and the destruction of the environment are not isolated examples of 'backward-looking' thinking and behaviour, but part of a longer tradition of self-help and cultural resistance without which 'sustainable development' has no contemporary meaning.

Chapter Two
The Earth Summit

In 1992 the United Nations Conference on Environment and Development (UNCED) took place in Rio de Janeiro. This chapter traces the recent history of international environmental policy before and after the 'Earth Summit'. It examines the tortuous trail by which the environment and development came to be considered together. Within the narrative we can discern issues in the sociology of ideas, and in science policy, that have frequently been eclipsed by events. The economic policies of the 1980s – the 'adjustment decade' – were rarely linked to the course of international environmental policy. Development aid was only belatedly linked to environmental goals. 'Green conditionality', itself a burden for the South, was, I shall argue, an attempt to force a late marriage between development and environmental objectives.

One of the principal thrusts of *Agenda 21*, and the national-level consultation exercises which should assist governments in meeting the 1992 guidelines established at the Earth Summit, is active local participation in environmental decision-making. As we shall see, particularly in Chapter Eight, local mobilisation around environmental issues is inextricably linked to wider, global, issues. Ultimately, the way we view sustainability within each country's own economic strategy will be decisive evidence of our national commitment to the new international agenda. The difficulty, and the challenge, is to make the connections between environmental and economic policy at both national and international levels. The lesson of the last decade is that if we wait for others to act before acting ourselves, we will lose momentum.

INTERNATIONAL ENVIRONMENTAL POLICY: THE ROAD FROM STOCKHOLM

To understand the present situation we need to take a few steps backwards (see Box 2.1). We might begin with the immediate post-war situation, when the Bretton Woods institutions were established. However, the 'modern' era of international environmental policy really commences with the Stockholm Conference on the Human Environment in 1972 which, among other things, led to the establishment of the United Nations Environment Programme (UNEP).

The development discourse reached its zenith in the 1960s. Although in Latin America there was growing unease with the idea of a sequential process of development, passing from the developed to the developing world, on the whole, development was still considered as relatively unproblematic, the major goal of the developing countries, and was cast very much in the image of what the industrialised world had achieved. At Stockholm in 1972 many of the representatives of the 'South' struck what was seen as a discordant note: the developed countries wanted to protect the environment, but to do so implied placing unnecessary checks on the progress of the developing countries. The environmental agenda, they said, was the agenda of what was later called the 'North'.

At the same time in the industrialised countries there was growing unease about the course that development was taking, and what were beginning to be perceived as the threats in store for the environment. *Limits to Growth*, which was published in 1972, gave expression to these fears. In the analysis of the Meadows team which wrote the report, the problem lay in the profligate use of natural resources. The resource base was limited, but our needs in the course of development were unlimited. The limits to growth were set by the seemingly exponential expansion of human needs, and consumption, against a fixed, unalterable supply of resources.

The idea that *scarcity* of natural resources, rather than a marked expansion in the uses to which we put them, should mark our undoing is, with hindsight, rather quaint. We should remember, however, that this was before the impact of the new high-yielding cereal varieties

---

Box 2.1 International environmental policy: benchmarks

Date	Events	Publications
1971	Man and Biosphere (MAB) launched	*Limits to Growth*
1972	UN Conference on Human Environment (Stockholm)	
1973		*Small is Beautiful*
1973/74	First Oil 'Shock' (4×)	
1979	Second Oil 'Shock'	*Progress for a Small Planet*
1980	Brandt (North–South) Commission World Conservation Strategy	
1982	Mexican default: debit crisis grows stabilisation structural adjustment policies	*Global 2000 Report*
1987	Brundtland Commission	*Our Common Future*
1989		*Pearce Report (Blueprint One)*
1990	Global Environmental Facility created IPCC reports	
1991		*Our Own Agenda (Latin America)*
	Second World Conservation Strategy UNCED Prepcoms meet	*Caring for the Earth*
1992	UNCED Earth Summit in Rio	*Agenda 21*
	GEF enhanced/Commission for Sustainable Development	

---

had been felt (the 'Green Revolution') and, of course, before the oil 'shocks' of the 1970s forced unwelcome adjustments on the world economy. The early 1970s were marked by a growing acknowledgement that development was 'historically determined'. It would not proceed in the same way in the South as it had in the North. The writings of Schumacher and Barbara Ward, the establishment of the International Institute for Environment and Development (IIED), laid emphasis on the importance of 'appropriate' technology and the *dis*economies of scale. Prometheus, if not quite 'chained', was at least put into a harness.

During the rest of the decade, attention shifted, at least in the North, to the economic, and increasingly financial, problems which accompanied the success of the OPEC countries in raising the price of oil. The most lasting effect, which was to send its long shadow into the next decade, was the accumulation of 'petrodollars' in Northern banks: capital in search of a home. The way in which these funds were released on the world market was to be the trigger for economic collapse, and the subsequent restructuring of the second half of the 1980s.

In 1980 two reports were published with a global remit. They bore little similarity to each other. The 'Brandt Report' (1980) devoted merely a few pages to the impending environmental crisis, although what was written showed extraordinary prescience. The World Conservation Strategy, also published in 1980, barely discussed the global economic issues that were so unsettling at the time. The Strategy did, however, focus minds around the connections between environmental problems and economic development. Much more effectively than the Man and Biosphere (MAB) programme, which had been launched almost a decade earlier, the World Conservation Strategy called for an alliance between natural and social scientists. Environmental problems could not be addressed effectively without hard economic and political decisions being taken. Watershed forests, extensive grasslands, coastal zones, could only be protected if their utilisation was 'sustainable', which it rarely was. Again, with hindsight (assisted by the second World Conservation Strategy, *Caring for the Earth*), the first World Conservation Strategy seems politically naive. Its strength was almost in this naivety, however. It read like a call to arms, unleashing idealism and commitment at a time when the orthodox development paradigm in the social sciences was under siege from the Left, and fewer thinking people kept faith with the goal of universal development.

In August 1982 the outgoing Mexican government of Lopez Portillo admitted publicly that it was unable to meet its debt obligations. The Mexican economy would have to be rescued. In Latin America, and elsewhere in the developing world, governments were forced to admit similar problems. The rise in interest rates which, as we shall see, was partly stimulated by North American re-armament, placed an impossible burden on countries which, a few years earlier, were being offered attractive loans by banks overburdened with 'surplus' funds. For many people in the South, the retrenchment that followed confirmed their worst fears; international capitalism was using dependent debtor countries to bring stability to the economies of the North. Environmental problems took a back seat during most of the 1980s. The dominant discourse was that of stabilisation and adjustment. The publication of *Global 2000* in 1982, however, had provided documentary evidence of the extent to which the global environment was being placed in jeopardy by economic policies. It also, and not incidentally, provided examples of global modelling for environmental change, which were later to take root within the scientific community and in North American policy circles. In many respects *Global 2000* marks the watershed between two epochs: one in which economic development and the environment were separate discourses and another in which attempts were made to bring them together.

The catalyst for doing so, of course, was the crisis in the global economy, which had seen capital flight on an unprecedented scale, made debtors of relatively strong economies, and turned the hopes of development through import substitution, in countries as different as Mexico and India, into failed promises accompanied by what sounded like empty rhetoric.

COUNSEL OF DESPAIR: INTERNATIONAL ENVIRONMENTAL PROBLEMS IN THE 1980S

The economic problems that dictated events throughout the 1980s had important implications for the way in which international environmental policy is viewed today. Current concerns with placing monetary values on the environment date from this period, as does the attempt to make the successful achievement of environmental goals an aspect of economic conditionality. I will argue that a third question is of even greater importance, but much more frequently neglected. This is the extent to which economic restructuring in the 1980s served to disempower the poor, not simply in terms of the political resources at their command, but also in terms of the legitimacy of their cultural vision and epistemologies. Before considering the legacy of the adjustment decade, for the environment and social processes at the international level, we need to explore the relationship between the economic crisis and the way it altered perceptions of global environmental management. If we want to understand the emphasis at UNCED, and subsequently on the development of principles for global environmental management, we should consider the circumstances in which the environmental agenda was formulated. We can begin with the economic context.

As we have seen, the first 1973/74 oil shock left the developing countries with significant trade imbalances which, initially, the International Monetary Fund (IMF) sought to address through stabilisation policies. The IMF's role was later replaced by that of the commercial banks. Between 1973 and 1981, private financial institutions increased their lending to less developed countries (LDCs) (excluding oil exporters) sixfold to $220 billion (US). By 1981, 7 per cent of the developing countries' debts were to the commercial banking sector. These commercial banks had little development expertise and poor control of lending policy, compared with that of the IMF.

By the 1970s too, LDC commodity prices were beginning to fall, and this, together with the second oil shock (1978–80) had adverse effects on their terms of trade. In addition, under President Reagan, renewed defence expenditure in the US pushed up interest rates to previously unheard-of levels. As global interest rates rose, most LDCs were forced to allocate a rising proportion of their dwindling foreign exchange to servicing their debts.

The economic crises of the 1980s led many LDCs to reduce their imports significantly, while seeking to stimulate export earnings against the tide of negative terms of trade. Chapter Five discusses the environmental effects of this squeeze on resource systems. Domestically the policies of the developing countries made greater inroads on capital investment in the early 1980s than on public expenditure per se. One of the consequences was that the majority of the poor, especially the rural poor, were unprotected at a time of fiscal discipline. To varying degrees, social spending fell in virtually all developing countries during the early 1980s. As the Latin American response to the Brundtland Report (WCED 1987) made clear, *Our Own Agenda* (IBRD 1991) was as far from being enacted at the end of the 1980s as it was a decade earlier.

The difference between the stabilisation policies encouraged largely by the IMF in the 1970s and the adjustment policies encouraged by the World Bank in the 1980s, was that the latter were supposed to rest on enhancing the supply side, through institutional reform and economic growth. The aim was to make economies more competitive in world markets where earlier reforms had emphasised reducing subsidies for products and services, as well as the scale of the public sector. Increasingly, stabilisation was associated with demand management, and it was left to the World Bank to provide the alternative economic package.

In its efforts to remove obstacles to economic growth in the early 1980s, the World Bank sought to reduce export taxes and to remove import quotas, which had previously impeded competitiveness on world markets. The Bank also sought to reform public enterprises. Without the expectation of a revival in the global economy the attention of the Bank switched to institutional reforms in the South, particularly sectoral adjustment loans. The agenda included reforming the manufacturing sector during the late 1980s and, as privatisation spread, reforming the financial sector in the hope of attracting foreign capital.

The adverse effects of the IMF's earlier adjustment policies on the poor produced some important responses from within the UN system. First among these was a report from UNICEF, which provided carefully documented cases of the impact of adjustment on children in developing countries. Despite some misgivings, the World Bank still insisted that during the transitional period adjustment could be expected to carry heavy costs, particularly for the poor, which only long-term improved economic performance could mitigate. One of the lessons of this period, of enormous consequence for meeting future environmental objectives, was the late recognition that countries needed to 'own' their adjustment programmes, if they were to prove at all effective.

Indeed, with hindsight, it seems strange that structural-adjustment lending in the 1980s did not incorporate environmental factors. There were several reasons for this, which include:

- the World Bank and other multilateral development banks (MDBs) did not view the environment as a priority investment at the time;
- borrowing countries had not requested financial support to deal with environmental problems;
- public concern with global environmental problems had not reached the point at which policy changes were considered necessary – in the 1980s, environmental costs were seen, on balance, as a natural consequence of economic growth;
- the connection between economic policy instruments and their environmental impacts was only poorly understood by the World Bank – often it was thought necessary to 'get the prices right' and everything else would take care of itself;

- environmental spending appeared to require more budgetary
  outlays and increased public expenditure, which ran counter to
  the whole thrust of adjustment lending (Reed 1992).

In many countries the failure to appreciate the environmental
consequences of adjustment policy was linked to the view taken of
economic policy reform, which was essentially short-term, and linked
to existing market conditions.

However, evidence began to grow that the supposed economic
benefits of adjustment policy would be undermined by a reduction
in the sustainability of the resource systems on which economic
growth depends. Population increase, in the context of reduced
resource-carrying capacity, was likely to exacerbate the social and
political tensions which adjustment policy brought in its train.
Economic policy reform would leave the poorest social groups more
exposed. This, in turn, further exacerbated the environmental consequences. The subsequent accelerated boost given to environmental
economics, by the World Bank and other development agencies,
reflected unease with the social consequences of adjustment policies,
and apprehension about the evidence of mounting environmental
problems.

Environmental economics was also given a boost by the publication, in 1987, of the Brundtland Commission's Report, *Our Common
Future* (WCED 1987). The Report caught the imagination of many
because of its insistence that science and technology could be utilised
to meet human goals. Sustainable development meant a commitment
to social and political ideals, rather than an abstract, ecocentric
'environmentalism'. The Report also recognised the contribution of
the non-governmental organisations to meeting environmental
objectives. Unlike previous reports, the Brundtland Commission
argued that successful environmental management was a means to
human fulfilment, rather than an end in itself. It also marked the point
at which policy discourse on the environment adopted economic
mechanisms as significant policy tools. As we have seen, this
effectively opened the door to an environmental economics which
sought to fill the policy vacuum.

The publication in the United Kingdom of the 'Pearce Report',
Blueprint For a Green Economy, (Pearce et al 1989) prompted the
suggestion that the real costs of environmental degradation could be
assigned in the development process through an evaluation of
environmental costs and benefits forsaken. The challenge was to
design policy instruments which could guide human behaviour,

through fiscal incentives rather than regulation alone, and encourage individuals to act more sustainably. This fitted well with a neo-liberal outlook on markets, in which individual preferences and the pursuit of free trade followed logically from stabilisation and structural adjustment. However, Goodland and Daly (1992), in a paper published by the World Bank, have argued that the accelerated deregulation which forms part of the Uruguay GATT round will prove prejudicial to the achievement of sustainability. Their case has two convincing elements. First, the GATT aims to maximise welfare gains from *trade*, rather than *total* welfare gains. The gains to welfare from the domestic production of non-traded goods and the maintenance of natural capital stock are not part of the GATT equation. Second, the prices that operate under 'free trade' do not reflect social and environmental costs. As they put it:

> Until the price of traded goods reflects their full environmental and social costs in each trading country, unregulated trade will undermine efficient national policies of internalizing external cost.
>
> (Goodland and Daly 1992, 7)

> Would it not make more sense for Third World countries to focus more on transforming their *own* resources into products for their *own* people, rather than exporting them to the North in exchange for consumer goods for Southern elites?
>
> (Goodland and Daly 1992)

Sentiments such as these, emanating from senior staff working within the Bank's mandate, suggest that the environmental discourse, once captured by the world's leading development institution, could be employed to challenge the new market economies, as well as to support them.

UNCED: THE ROAD TO RIO

Watching the media coverage of the United Nations Conference on Environment and Development at Rio de Janeiro in 1992 one could be excused for thinking that the principal environmental problems facing the globe were climate change, the loss of forests and, with them, biodiversity. There was very little coverage of the underlying problems which affect most human beings in their daily lives. *The*

Economist complained that population was 'the issue that Rio forgot'. However, it was not the only neglected issue, since there was little discussion, and less coverage, of a number of other important questions, notably trade, poverty and the continuing debt crisis in the South. With hindsight we may come to see UNCED as marking an important shift away from the development discourse of the 1970s and 1980s, towards a new concern with science and uncertainty, a concern that paralysed Northern governments by laying bare the contradictions of their development. The 'success' of development, including improved material standard of living, had not necessarily brought improvements in the quality of life, as measured by personal security, freedom from pollution and traffic congestion, and risks from nuclear and toxic waste streams.

The environmental concerns of the 1990s have proved to be about the implications of profligacy, of plenty, rather than the limits to growth. The attention of the world came to rest not on the resources which made growth possible, but on the way that we dispose of the products of that growth, the way that policy adapts to 'sinks' (Redclift 1995, Brown and Adger 1993).

What was the 'state of the world' in June 1992 when the world's leaders met in Rio?

- More than two hundred million people were estimated to depend upon increasingly vulnerable forest resources.
- Eight hundred million people were affected by serious land degradation in dryland areas of the world.
- More than one billion people relied on fragile irrigation systems, plagued by problems of unreliable water supply and soil salinisation.
- Five hundred million people occupied degraded watersheds.
- Four hundred million people were vulnerable to the resulting downstream siltation from these watersheds.
- An estimated one billion people lacked adequate, safe water for their own consumption.
- Almost two billion people suffered from either malnutrition or the lack of proper sanitation, *and each year thirteen and a half million children died as a result.* Two million of these children, under five years old, died from malaria.
- Over one billion of the world's population lived in cities where air pollution was below World Health Organization standards, and *each day* thirty-five thousand children died from environmentally related diseases.

- Almost one billion people lived in cities where emissions of sulphur dioxide exceeded safe standards. (*World Development Report* 1992).

This was the very alarming context in which treaties were being prepared for signature at Rio. As I shall argue, the neglect of poverty, and distributional issues generally, has served to cast a long shadow over what was agreed at UNCED. It promises to be a shadow that will be difficult to cast off in the wake of the Rio agreements.

One of the things that distinguished the Rio conference from earlier meetings, including the deliberations of the World Commission for Environment and Development (Brundtland Commission), was the level of preparation. Before UNCED was convened there were meetings of various working groups and preparatory meetings (prepcoms) intended to establish the agenda, and agreement about what was known and not known. At these meetings information was requested on a large number of environmental factors which made development unsustainable. It was information-gathering, rather than the formulation of policies to combat problems, which was the focus of attention.

These discussions gave rise to a number of problems, which were to emerge later at the conference itself (IIED 1992).

First, the discussions on climate change were highly divisive. In the view of most Southern countries the focus needed to be on the transfer of cleaner technologies from the North, particularly for energy generation. This, in turn, raised the question of ways in which such transfers could be funded: the vexed question of 'additionality'. There was also some discussion of the procedures for evaluating the costs of 'mitigating' the effects of climate change. Various countries from the South (the G77 group) argued that climate agreements should precede the Forest Agreement, that the conference would need to tackle the causes of climate change first, rather than negotiate about the conservation of sinks, in the form of tropical forests. Such differences, of course, struck at the different underlying orientations of the developed and developing countries: the former to prioritise climate in defence of their development achievements, the latter to urge a different form of development on the North.

Second, the discussions surrounding biodiversity proved to be much more difficult than some observers had expected. There were problems of definition, as biodiversity and biotechnology were very closely related issues. For the countries of the South with rich biodiversity, particularly wrapped up in tropical forests, there was a need to protect their resources, and their sovereignty, from the depredations of transnational companies located in the North.

In the view of most countries with large tropical forests, the search for biological materials involved the privatisation of what were, in fact, common property resources. These sentiments were echoed by some non-governmental organisations, and lobbyists in the North, for whom the ownership of nature was a political issue at least as important as the possession of global sinks.

Third, the preparatory meetings witnessed considerable discussion about the disposal of hazardous wastes, another issue which seemed to highlight the increasingly important sink functions of the developing world. Sensitivities in this area were underlined by remarks attributed to a senior World Bank employee, Lawrence Summers, which implied that it was logical, on economic grounds, for richer countries to dispose of their wastes in the poorer countries, whose costs were lower. The discussions of hazardous wastes, prior to UNCED, focused on the feasibility of a global ban on their export to developing countries, and the increasingly urgent (with the dissolution of the Soviet Union) problem of disposing of radioactive wastes. Again, evidence was beginning to appear of mutually incompatible demands: from the North, that market forces should govern the disposal of wastes; from the South, that the developed countries should begin by cleaning up their act.

The fourth set of issues to surface in the preparations for UNCED struck at the very different perspectives of Northern and Southern governments. The G77 countries supported the idea that the Earth Summit should report on both development and the environment. It would be important, therefore, to consider ways of raising living standards in the developing world. They requested that population be left out of the Rio deliberations, particularly the linkages between population growth and the environment. The developed countries (G7) insisted that population was retained as an issue, reflecting their concern that increased levels of consumption in the larger countries of the South posed the problem of accelerated global warming.

There were heated discussions over responsibility for global environmental change: the North arguing that population was the driving force behind climate change, while the South insisted that 'over-consumption' in the North, at globally unsustainable levels, imperilled the survival of the world's poor. Linking these questions was the choice of mechanisms to affect a shift in the global imbalances. The transfer of cleaner technologies, for example, involved transferring financial resources to the developing countries, through the Global Environment Facility (GEF) (which was established in 1990) and there was a request for new sources of funding to be identified, before the conference convened. These issues, of the way technology is shared, and the financial mechanisms for ensuring that the South's role in global conservation was recognised, proved to be of enormous importance during, and in the aftermath of, Rio.

The process that led to Rio was initiated by the Brundtland Commission, with public fora being held in Bangkok, Mexico City, Cairo, Buenos Aires and Amsterdam, between February and May 1992. There was considerable participation from the non-governmental organisations (NGOs), which sought to mobilise opinion around the production of national reports, in advance of the meetings. These wide consultations between governments and NGOs led to the Global Forum at Rio, which paralleled the official meeting of governments' representatives. However, it should be noted that divisions within the ranks of NGOs became more apparent, as their public profile grew. O'Keefe, Middleton and Moyo (1993) make the point that the definition of what constituted an NGO was extraordinarily wide, including international businesses and, indeed, any organisation outside the public sector. By the time UNCED was convened, the expectations for the conference far exceeded its mandate which was, as the International Institute for Environment and Development declared, 'not . . . very workable' (IIED 1992, 3).

THE UNCED DELIBERATIONS: CONVENTIONS AND A NEW AGENDA

Climate Change

In a meticulously documented and persuasive report, initially to the Dutch government, Krause, Bach and Kooney argued:

> Much of the current climate warming debate still proceeds along the narrow lines of conventional air pollution abatement policy. But climate stabilization is an entirely different challenge. The greenhouse effect is driven by a confluence of environmental impacts that have their source not only in the nature of human resource use, but also in the nature of the current international economic order. Climate stabilization *therefore requires a comprehensive turn around towards environmentally sound and socially*

equitable development – in short, an unprecedented North–South compact on sustainable development.

(Krause, Bach and Kooney 1990, 1.7–1, emphasis added)

The failure of the Rio meeting was, ultimately, a failure to recognise this relationship. Consequently, the omission of serious discussion about international debt, poverty and trade, as well as the failure to address population, served to undermine workable agreement on the issue of climate.

The discussion of climate was hamstrung by the very different perspectives of different groupings of countries. Large developing countries, like China and India, refused to be thwarted in their efforts to develop, and to improve the living standards of their vast, and very poor, populations. The US, and to a lesser extent the European Union, sought to limit the effect of any international undertakings to curtail economic growth, which were viewed as politically inadmissible, as far as their domestic audience was concerned.

The governments subscribing to OPEC (Organisation of Petroleum Exporting Countries) clearly wanted to play a major part in managing the world's dependence on fossil fuels, and did not favour transitional measures to move away from dependence upon them. The small island states of the Pacific and Caribbean, in the front line of any projected sea-level rise, nonetheless possessed very little political influence. The countries of sub-Saharan Africa were poorly represented at Rio, and even following the Nairobi Declaration (1990) viewed the climate negotiations as of relatively marginal interest. Within the South it was the so-called newly industrialising countries (NICs), such as Korea, Taiwan and Singapore, which were most ambivalent about the climate negotiations. As O'Keefe et al (1994) argue, following the World Development Report (IBRD 1992) Singapore and Hong Kong, between them, dispose of as much toxic wastes as the whole of sub-Saharan Africa.

Initially the (then) European Community had sought to advance the idea of a unilateral carbon tax, as an instrument for enforced energy efficiency. However, this proposal failed when a 'conditionality' clause was inserted into the documentation, requiring other developed countries to comply, before the measure could be accepted. Japan and the United States both opposed the idea of a carbon tax, the latter government weakening the treaty further by refusing to endorse timetables for action, and targets for greenhouse-gas emissions.

In the event forty-three countries signed the climate change treaty at Rio, but the targets for reduced emissions are unlikely to be achieved, even with increased energy efficiency under the existing policy options. Other instruments, such as an international carbon tax, or the introduction of tradeable permits, would provide elegant ways in which countries with high fossil-fuel consumption could manage the transition towards greater energy efficiency and a larger stage in renewables. It is extremely unlikely that tradeable permits will be employed since they imply transfers in the order of $50 billion per year, from the richer industrialised countries to those of the South (Bertram 1992). Such a transfer would go some way to achieving the objectives of sustainable development in the UNCED communiques.

The Treaty sets as a target the stabilisation of Northern emissions of greenhouse gases at 1990 levels by the year 2000. Success in achieving these targets is to be reported to the Conference of the Parties, which met initially in 1995, on the basis of an internal audit, rather than an external assessment. There are still difficult problems surrounding any external audit or verification. The Treaty does allow for stronger measures to be taken internationally, if the threat of global warming is seen to increase. However, since the interpretation of this threat is likely to continue to be contested in the near future, there is little immediate likelihood that the provisions will be tightened.

The problems that accompany a comprehensive and workable treaty on climate have been discussed at length in the literature (see Grubb et al (1993) for a definitive version of the agreements themselves). Among the most important are the following:

1. The Framework Climate Convention does provide a 'framework' for future action, if governments want to use it. They are not compelled to do so by the agreements entered into. The question remains: how can treaty commitments be made binding? As Grubb et al argue:

> Thus it remains unclear how many aspects of the Climate Convention will operate in practice, and it can only be seen as an important first step on a very long road. The process of negotiating the Convention itself had an impact, both in educating many different countries, and in pushing concerned countries towards making and explaining commitments.
>
> (Grubb et al 1993, 72)

2. One of the few sanctions that might be employed against 'free-
    riders' in the future is some form of trade embargo. However, if
    international environmental treaties use trade measures as
    disincentives to free-riding then these measures will inevitably act
    as selective restrictions on imports, which (like the importation
    of goods produced 'unfairly') will contravene the General
    Agreement on Tariffs and Trade (GATT). It is unlikely, then, that
    a climate agreement with effective powers of sanction can precede
    major new reforms in the GATT. As Paul Ekins has put it:

    > If the potential environmental benefits of free trade are to be
    > realised, trading rules, such as those developed by GATT, must
    > recognise that environmental externalities are in effect environ-
    > mental subsidies (that are as economically distorting and unfair
    > as any financial subsidy) and that environmental externalities
    > are pervasive.
    >
    > (Ekins 1993, 5)

Forest Principles

Moving from the climate negotiations to the deliberations
surrounding the declaration of Forest Principles, it is clear that, once
again, the division between the interests of North and South was
apparent. The principle behind any kind of financial transfer to
tropical forest countries was that preserving forests has a global
environmental benefit, which is not wholly captured by the host
country. The industrialised countries could then be expected to
transfer funds to poorer countries like Brazil or Indonesia, which
possess large tropical forest reserves.

The background against which these negotiations took place was
the much-discredited Tropical Forestry Action Plan, developed within
the United Nations system. Opposition to this Plan from international
NGOs and many developing countries was marked. Any agreement
to manage tropical forests in the global interest was likely to meet
with objections from countries which, rightly, saw this as an infringe-
ment of their sovereignty. At the same time, financial compensation
to such countries soon encounters problems of so-called
'additionality', which have dogged the role of the Global Environment
Facility (GEF). Additionality is the principle that, to obtain
environmental funds, countries have to demonstrate that 'global'
problems represent a cost additional to those which all countries

bear. As Jordan has observed, without a real commitment to sustainable development within their borders, there is little prospect of more funds being allocated to protecting the global environment:

> At heart, the North is deeply opposed to providing new finance unless its self-interest is clearly guaranteed, whereas parts of the South simply lack the capability to cope effectively with a vast influx of new capital ... one suspects that, at root, there are very deep differences in the way that the North and the South perceive the need for, and likely role of, additional financial transfers. The developed states seem to regard them as a price (to be minimized if at all possible) to be paid for enlisting the support of the South in tackling common problems. Meanwhile, the developing states seek to maximize transfers, arguing that they are a rightful and legitimate means to address the inequities in the operation of the world economy.
>
> (Jordan 1994, 20–21).

The eventual outcome of the discussions of Forest Principles was a non-binding and unclear set of propositions, which were opposed by leading developing countries, notably Malaysia and India. The G77 (developing) countries argued that they would sign away part of their sovereignty only in exchange for effective compensation for the revenue they would be forgoing. Eventually a compromise was brokered by the German Environment Minister, but unlike the Climate Change and Biodiversity Conventions, no timetable was agreed, and the resulting document was not binding.

Biodiversity

The outcome of the discussions surrounding biodiversity was rather different, in that in this case it was the industrialised world, principally the United States, which sought to advance its claim to acquire resources owned by another state. The developing countries wanted to control biodiversity as a means of protecting their stake in natural capital, and the income that this might provide. The North, on the other hand, wanted access to biodiversity for commercial profit, and particularly for the development of a research capacity in biotechnology. The United States felt the Treaty compromised its biotechnology industries, and refused to sign it.

Several options were put forward for breaking this inevitable deadlock:

1. non-profit institutes in the North might contract for the use of wild genetic material, for commercial fees, or through sharing revenue;
2. private companies might support national scientific institutes in the South, in return for exclusive rights to screen biological collections;
3. host governments might exploit resources, and foreign companies could be granted exploratory concessions by them.

The problem was: how can host communities acquire rights which translate into incentives to conserve biodiversity? This would either require large-scale international finance, dwarfing the modest proposed budget of the Global Environment Facility (GEF) or it would leave commercial operators free to exploit the market. In the event, after nearly four years of negotiation, the Biodiversity Treaty was approved only in a much modified form. President Bush failed to ratify the Treaty, with the words that 'the American way of life is not up for negotiation'. Agreement on long-term funding has subsequently been delayed. The Treaty had already been described by Mostafa Tolba, of the United Nations Environment Programme, as 'the minimum on which the international community can agree'.

IN THE WAKE OF RIO: INTERNATIONAL FINANCE AND POLITICAL DEVOLUTION

As Jordan has argued, the more specific the obligations to address global environmental issues, the more ambiguous and vague the commitments (Jordan 1994). It is one thing to have developed a broad consensus of opinion on the need to tackle the issues, and quite another to agree the formulas for funding the policy interventions that might ensue. We have seen how the commitments to part of the global agenda, referring to climate change and biodiversity losses in particular, principally reflect Northern concerns. The more fundamental questions for poor peoples' livelihoods in the foreseeable future, such as how to provide clean drinking water, or to reverse land degradation, reflect aspects of sustainable development which were on the margins of the Rio discussions.

Agenda 21 was the document which paid most attention to sustainable development at the grass-roots level, and to the calls for local management of resources. The UNCED Secretariat estimated that to implement Agenda 21 would require *additional* aid of approximately $125 billion (US) worldwide each year, from 1993 to 2000. The estimates of the World Bank were somewhat more than half this figure. In the event, despite the rhetoric in evidence at Rio, only about $2.5 billion (US) was actually pledged by the richer countries. At a long, pre-Rio negotiating session in New York, the French government had proposed that the European Union contribute $3.8 billion (US) to help pay for the implementation of Agenda 21. France's European partners were not easily convinced, and the scheme has effectively been abandoned.

Part of the problem in voting funds is that the institutions that manage them are scrutinised fairly closely. American environmentalists opposed the idea that the International Development Association, the soft-loans element of the World Bank, should gain funds under its periodic budget replenishment. Suspicion of the World Bank, or its subsidiaries, was widespread in non-governmental organisations, especially in the South. Many countries from among the G77 group wanted a 'green fund', financed by the North on an agreed formula, and based on an international carbon tax. However, opposition to this idea from the G7 countries was vociferous and this idea, too, was dropped.

The Global Environment Facility was formed before the UNCED conference. It was to be administered jointly by: the World Bank, which provided the expertise for investment projects; UNEP, which provided the secretariat; and the UNDP, for technical assistance and project identification. From the beginning, however, the GEF has been seen as the child of the World Bank.

The central principle behind the GEF's mandate was that of 'additionality'. The UNCED Secretariat suggested that the GEF could pay developing countries for the *extra cost* of policies to slow global warming, an idea which met opposition from the G7 countries. For many countries in the South there was little point in seeking to reach agreement on climate or biodiversity negotiations if the international economic order remained unchanged. For them the challenge was to redirect extensive funding towards the South, and to tackle essentially structural issues that impeded their sustainability.

The GEF itself reflected the position of the North. Voting rights in the GEF, like those for the World Bank, were heavily in favour of the developed countries. The staff of the GEF were recruited from the World Bank. Most importantly, however, the terms of reference for the GEF's work were essentially those agreed by the donor countries.

The remit of the GEF was exclusively with transnational environmental problems, such as transboundary pollution, and the loss of biodiversity, rather than the 'bread-and-butter' issues which concerned most of the developing world. In addition, the developing countries expressed the view that progress depended upon the cancellation of their debts. Without the cancellation of the debt they saw the demand for environmental good practice as, in effect, a form of conditionality, which would be used to ensure their compliance with the wishes of the donor countries.

As Jordan demonstrates, the vexed question of environmental additionality was inherited from the negotiations over the Montreal Protocol on ozone-depleting substances, signed in 1987, when countries like China and India acceded to the agreement because they saw the prospect of new funds (Interim Multilateral Ozone Fund) and financial inducements to clean technology transfer (Jordan 1994). In practice, however, the developed states favoured the Bretton Woods institutions (the World Bank and the International Monetary Fund) because they were deemed to be more efficient, and their work of more technical merit. They were also more accountable to their paymasters within the G7 community of nations. The work of the GEF would essentially bolster some of the activities with which the World Bank was already engaged, attaching a price to existing or augmented project funding. The wider aspirations of Agenda 21, and the search for sustainable development, could be politely forgotten.

Almost before the last government representatives had left Rio it became clear that the ambiguous wording of the agreements, and the exemptions granted individual states, would make it difficult to follow up even the rather tighter Framework Convention on Climate Change, and the Biodiversity Convention. Their management was entrusted to the GEF, but only on an interim basis. The existence of concrete funds with which to meet the additionality provisions, was soon put in jeopardy. As Jordan comments, 'at heart, the North is deeply opposed to providing new finances unless its self-interest is clearly guaranteed' (Jordan 1994, 20). Even the sums of money which remain contested, however, are so modest as to make no demonstrable difference to the problems they are designed to address. Even a sympathetic view of the GEF's work elicits the conclusion that without substantial debt relief, for example, little can be achieved within the terms agreed at Rio (Brown, Adger and Turner 1993).

In June 1994 the GEF reached the end of its three-year pilot stage. A 'replenishment' of about $2 billion (US) was proposed for its continuation. The future of the GEF was discussed at a meeting in Cartagena, Colombia in December 1993. An evaluation of the GEF's work reflected opposition from some G77 governments, and the continued doubts of environmental NGOs. The dilemma faced by the GEF is that it needs to reassure the North to retain any funding and credibility, without entirely losing the confidence of the G77 countries, whose consent to its activities is essential.

Against the wishes of the World Bank, the evaluation of the GEF suggested that all finance for new projects should be suspended until new guidelines were in place. The evaluation stated that the definition of 'incremental cost', to be met by the GEF, as 'the additional cost of protecting the environment of a country, over and above its domestic benefits', was insufficiently precise. Even more contentiously the idea has been put forward that GEF projects should not be initiated by the Bank, UNDP or UNEP, but at the regional and national levels of developing countries.

In addition, it was suggested that regional development banks, other United Nations agencies and environmental groups, should be able to compete for the GEF's funds, and that NGOs and developing-country governments should be more involved in the GEF's decisions. None of these suggestions is popular with the senior staff of the World Bank. The result has been a stalemate: the World Bank arguing that progress has been made in devising mechanisms to manage the new facility, while the developing-country representatives maintain that they are being offered less money and no effective managerial control. As one Latin American representative put it:

> offering money in exchange for control over an organism in which the North and the South should be partners shows us that there are still walls more difficult to tear down than the Berlin wall.
>
> (Raghavan 1993, 4)

GLOBAL ENVIRONMENTAL MANAGEMENT: A REALISTIC PERSPECTIVE

There are a number of responses to this question, most of them building on existing environmental practices, or seeking to develop new forms of collaboration within civil society.

First, there is little point in considering global environmental changes as unrelated to other global processes, such as the liberalisation of trade and the penetration of the media. Responding positively to the international agenda on the environment means establishing the connections between environmental benefits and other social and economic benefits and costs. The most active non-governmental organisations have sought to make these connections, in advancing the global environmental agenda. The activities of NGOs in Europe, and globally, have set the pace for international policy-making to a considerable degree. They have acted as the voice of civil society on these issues. However, they do not have the tax-raising and spending powers of governments, nor can they reach agreements on behalf of citizens, as governments do. The next phase of international agreements will require governments prepared to nurture and lead an active citizenship, rather than governments embarassed into action, and only willing to take action when there is a danger of being outflanked by allies, or adversaries.

At the international level this inevitably takes us back to some of the discussions prior to the UNCED meeting, to consider the role, for example, that 'debt forgiveness' might play in channelling resources towards sustainable development projects in the South. Britain has enormous expertise, unrivalled for a country of its size, in the technical and managerial aspects of project management and appraisal in developing countries. What is required is a commitment to exercise these skills on behalf of the developing nations.

Second, the global environmental policy agenda cannot be fashioned around a belief in impartial 'scientific' advice. It is true that some of the research institutions of science and technology perceive short-term benefits in the uncertainty surrounding global warming. However, it may be more difficult to reach agreement when the facts are uncertain, and heavily contested by different lobbies or 'stakeholders'. The answer is not to call for an end to uncertainty – or to wait until such an end is in sight – but to take preventative measures now, most of which are beneficial in the short-term. To be successful in such a strategy means enlisting the public, in a way never contemplated by governments outside wartime.

Third, the broadening of the debate about global change, and the increased involvement of the public, rests upon a process of democratisation, and a new definition of participatory citizenship. It may well be at the level of local government that this proves to be most important. It can certainly be argued that Agenda 21 has proved most useful as the basis for wide-ranging enquiry, on the part of local authorities themselves, into the best methods of increasing local-level sustainability. However, much closer links are needed between local voluntary groups, properly funded, statutory bodies and local government. To do so would not only demand a devolution of power and resources downwards, towards elected representatives and local organisations, but also a willingness to undertake a negotiation with several 'sides' to it. Some of the implications of responding to global pressures at the local level, while mounting an alternative sustainable agenda for political action, are discussed in Chapter Eight.

Perhaps the most important level at which progress can be made, however, is the one for which Britain shows least enthusiasm: that of the European Union. Liberatore (1993) has shown how the UK has failed to rise to the European challenge. She writes that:

> The European Community provides the unique example of a supranational setting since the EC legislation supersedes national legislation and an EC institution (the Commission) has regulatory competences ... the EC willingness to play a leading role is linked to the need to formulate an agreed position for the Community and its Member States.
>
> (Liberatore 1993, 15–16)

The strategy of the European Union, in response to the challenges of UNCED, consists of several parts, each of which require British endorsement.

1. The European Union can act in a leadership role internationally, both because of its size and the wealth of its constituent states, and because it has long recognised the need to curb the excesses of economic growth. The opportunity exists to play an enhanced collective role on the world stage. The move towards an internal market within the European Union is expressly linked to that of enhanced sustainability, for example, in meeting clean technology standards. The British government should welcome this commitment, rather than resenting control from Brussels.
2. The fulfilment of environmental, as well as social and economic, goals also presents real opportunities for investment in cleaner technologies, and for environmental protection measures which enhance economic competitiveness. Measures that form part of a 'no-regrets' strategy, such as the establishment of more ambitious targets for the stabilisation of emissions, measures aimed at increasing energy efficiency and the carbon-dioxide/energy tax, could form the basis of new global policy initiative. Instead, the UK expressed scepticism, even before UNCED, about the effects of such measures. In addition it partly shared the scepticism of the US towards the biodiversity convention, and the

need to increase development aid significantly (Liberatore 1993, 21).

3. In principle, at least, *Towards Sustainability*, the European Union's programme for sustainable development, and Fifth Environmental Action Programme, which was published in 1992, has a number of relatively innovative ingredients. It calls for preventative measures to deal with environmental problems, and identifies the failure of post-hoc environmental management. It also seeks to involve all sectors of society in the design of solutions to our current environmental problems.

These problems clearly extend beyond the nation state, and beyond regional groups like the European Union itself. Recognition that this involves responsibilities for governments, however, can be seen as an enormous policy opportunity: to put flesh on the bones of the Environmental Action Plan would be a significant new step.

FROM SCIENCE TO POLICY: ENVIRONMENTAL MANAGEMENT AND THE UNCED PROCESS

The Rio Conference raised the hopes of many, including both Northern and Southern NGOs. The way these hopes were subsequently dashed was reported exhaustively, if not always accurately, in the media. The North 'set out to secure the global environmental conventions it wanted' (Jordan 1993, 5). The South sought to exploit the only card it possessed: the threat of not acceding to the framework conventions that were negotiated. Issues of North/South transfer were never resolved at Rio. The pledges offered by the North as 'sweeteners' were just sufficient to find support in the South, but the offer of extra resources was, as Jordan (1993) indicates, both narrowly defined and contractually limited. By mid-1993, 31 countries had ratified the Climate Treaty, but they did not include the European Community.

The Global Environment Facility, which had started life before UNCED, existed to help finance transnational environmental policies, but will not address the environmental issues which remain priorities for the poorest developing countries. The GEF is supposed to meet only the 'incremental costs' of approved projects. The difficulty is that this is likely to mean that funded projects are not popular locally nor, in development banking terms, risk-worthy. Local property rights to nature are poorly defined, and global 'sovereignty' is still largely a rhetorical device. There is considerable evidence that the pledges offered by the North will remain just that: promises, rather than action. There has been a suggestion that the GEF will be more accountable, more democratically governed, than the other Bretton Woods institutions. It remains to be seen how much more democratic, and whether this reduces the GEF's mandate or budget. On the positive side, UNCED has forced the UN system to examine itself or be examined by outside assessors. It was also an occasion, as Arnaldo Gabaldon of Venezuela put it, 'when, unlike the debt rescheduling negotiations something could be said from *both* sides of the table'. Perhaps most importantly, the very fact that UNCED happened at all has given those involved in environmental disputes some armoury. As I argue elsewhere, in Mexico severe environmental problems or conflicts which were previously looked upon as parochial are now viewed from within a 'global' post-UNCED perspective (Redclift 1993). This has given confidence, for example, to Mexican environmentalists contesting toxic waste disposal, and other abuses, on the border with the US. The actions of companies and politicians are now set against the high moral ground of Rio declarations. At the same time it should be noted that the national state is quite capable of appropriating the sustainable develoment agenda within a highly authoritanian context, for example in the case of Burma (Parnwell and Bryant 1996).

The issue which took the Northern governments to Rio, of course, was climate change. The first reports of the Intergovernmental Panel for Climate Change (IPCC) provided sceptical opinion with very little reassurance. We still did not know precisely how or how much global warming would occur. We were still unclear about the link between changes in climatic systems and biological systems. The Global Circulation Models (GCMs) that were used to predict global climate change have many limitations and, more particularly, are unreliable guides to regional climate change and levels of precipitation. Nevertheless, the precautionary principle, or some variant of it, took root in some policy circles, and the scientific community galvanised itself for a new challenge and a new opportunity. More radical Green opinion consoled itself with the knowledge that environmental policy options based on 'least-cost' principles could gain political credibility. 'Uncertainty', always a feature of environmental policy discourse, was beginning to be recognised. It might be possible in future to challenge 'the facts' surrounding environmental issues, as environmental pressure groups frequently did, without seeming to abandon contingency planning.

The IPCC reports have matured into a 'second assessment' phase.

Their initial importance, in the run-up to Rio, cannot be exaggerated. The one thing which might bring the developed world to the conference table, and perhaps even the negotiating table, was the prospect of its own economic and social system being undermined. Unfortunately, this did not lead to the global consensus that many people wanted, which might have provided collaborative mechanisms for addressing sustainable development. The effect of IPCC was to heighten the gap between Northern concerns with the environment – 'post-modern environmental management' (Jordan 1993, 3) – and those of the South.

MAKING SENSE OF THE ENVIRONMENT/DEVELOPMENT DEBATE

An analysis of the last two decades of international policy on development and the environment leads to the following observations:

1. It is clear that economic policies, like those of structural adjustment, were intended to address macro-level problems for the economies concerned. No account was taken, in their design and implementation, of their effect at the micro-level, particularly the household. The environmental impact of these policies remains ill-defined; certainly none was anticipated when they were formulated. At the same time, the way that households and communities manage natural resources remains a key to more successful environmental management. It is the local level that matters most.
2. It is also clear that environmental management has taken a very large step in the last five years or so. The canvas is now a global one, partly because some changes in the environment are clearly systemic, indeed global, in nature. Most of the machinery of environmental management is local in design, and reflects specific traditions of land use and conservation policy, notably in the United Kingdom and North America. Under the Man and the Biosphere Programme (MAB), 'Biosphere Reserves' were established in the 1970s. Today, however, international agreements are being proposed to manage not only Common Property Resources, but a plethora of other environmental goods and services: gas emissions, waste disposal, biodiversity conservation. In this case the micro-level has been the model for macro-level, ultimately global, policies. Can such levels be breached?

The provenance of economic and environmental policy interventions helps explain the difficulties that beset international negotiations. In the view of the North most of the economies of the South need to learn a lesson from the newly industrialising 'tigers' of East Asia (see Chapter Four). India, for example, is today faced with structural adjustment policies like those that Latin America experienced in the 1980s. Sub-Saharan Africa, already in a parlous state, has been further undermined by structural adjustment and shifts in the international terms of trade. Western Europe and the United States are locked in conflicts over agricultural protection. There are very few new 'tigers' in the ring, although there is considerable evidence, as we shall see in Chapter Four, that environmental problems in Asia will grow more severe.

In the view of most Southern countries, we have not even begun to address the real issues behind environment and development. Thirteen *million* children under five years of age die needlessly, from poor sanitation and the diseases linked to poverty. From a Southern perspective, particularly that of the poorest countries, concern with climate change and biodiversity is necessarily linked to poverty and the international economic system. The dispute between Anil Agarwal and the World Resources Institute last year, ostensibly about the interpretation and use of data, illustrates this difference perfectly (Agarwal and Narain 1991).

Workable policies for sustainable development will falter unless international agreements reach beyond the tentative Framework Conventions that are being ratified at the moment. What is required is the restructuring of economic relations to meet sustainability criteria. At the moment, those of the United Kingdom reflect a set of assumptions about existing high levels of production and consumption. These will have to be reassessed. There is also a need, as Agenda 21 acknowledges, to bring reflexivity to environmental management: to be prepared to learn how to incorporate sustainability criteria as we go along.

During a recession, particularly, economic issues assume more importance in the public consciousness, and the political profile of the environment recedes. This is happening in the UK today. However, by making sustainability an essential, and positive, component of economic policy, there is a good chance that some of the momentum of the last decade will not be lost. Real progress in reaching more sustainable development at the international level rests on the measures we are prepared to take in the UK, as everywhere. More than anything, we need to explore the interactions between policies in traditionally separated areas of concern to ensure a coherent, workable programme for sustainability.

We need to look at the whole spectrum of policies: the design of our energy policies, the development of an integrated transport policy to release people from dependence on the private car, housing policies which involve people in the design and management of their built environment, and food policies which lead to a healthier diet, and to agricultural systems which are more sustainable worldwide. And we need to do all these things while living within environmental targets set by our own consumption, and our own capacity to manage our wastes.

Chapter Three

Meeting Environmental Targets

Since the Earth Summit, held in Rio de Janeiro in 1992, the world has set itself some demanding environmental targets. For example, Article Two of the Framework Climate Convention states that greenhouse gases need to be stabilised at a level which prevents dangerous interference with the climate system, and within a time frame which allows ecosystems to adapt successfully. Essentially, the world is being set environmental targets through reference to physical processes which we are only beginning to understand.

This has raised problems for science. At what point does the speed with which climate change occurs prevent ecosystem adaptation? We do not know the answer to this question. It is virtually impossible to establish critical thresholds, or levels, at which natural systems can adapt successfully to climate. It is also important to point out that human societies have to determine what an 'acceptable' level of tolerance would be. At what point does the range of greenhouse gas forcing, that can be accommodated by a natural system, become acceptable to us? What degree of stress, or pressure, on natural systems should we tolerate? And who, exactly, is doing the tolerating?

Scientific problems are matched, indeed enhanced, by those of policy. How can stabilisation (of climate) be achieved? How can ecosystem considerations be built into stabilisation policies? Much of the voluminous literature on sustainable development, particularly since the Brundtland Commission reported in 1987, has sought to establish workable definitions which can be used as criteria, or even targets, for policy.

On the whole, however, those who advocate greater sustainable development do so on a precautionary basis, in the belief that we do not know (and may never know) the exact relationship between human economic activities and their environmental consequences. Research in the social sciences has proceeded along a rather different path from most of the natural sciences, in seeking to establish feasible measures which might reduce the threat of global warming (among other things) while carrying short- and medium- term advantages. Environmental policy, often correctly in my view, is usually presented as a so-called 'win–win' situation.

This does not remove from us the responsibility for understanding how human societies might adapt to environmental constraints, including physical changes which have been enhanced by human actions and interference. We need to understand the consequences of our actions for the environment, both in terms of resource depletion and degradation, and the pressures placed on sinks. But as social scientists we also need to explore the commitments which we have to our economic and social models. This takes us into a different domain in Chapter Seven, a different frontier, in which the way that we understand and manage the environment is seen as a response to social behaviour and values.

This book is written in the belief that understanding the relationship between physical processes and human actions, sources and sinks, means more than charting a traffic in materials. It also means assessing our behaviour in terms of its implications for the 'natural' environment, adopting a perspective that, while acknowledging that the environment is socially constructed, insists that the construction we place on the environment can influence the constraints placed on us. As we will see in Chapter Six, faced by a traffic in materials, our models might also provide a traffic in ideas.

GLOBAL ENVIRONMENTAL CHANGE

Anthropogenic (human-driven) changes in the global environment need to be understood within an even larger compass: that of the natural systems of the Earth. Since time immemorial, human beings have altered, indeed managed, their natural environments. In the era before industrialisation humans used the natural ecosystem for food, clothing and the materials they needed for building structures, dwellings and farms. They also mined the planet for minerals and metals with which to make weapons, tools and, ultimately, coins, the means of exchange. Most of the utensils which human societies produced from nature were not consumed quickly, they were used and re-used for decades, even centuries.

The Industrial Revolution which began in Britain in the late eighteenth century, changed all this. Prior to industrialisation, the only unsustainable losses from human economic activity were forest cover and topsoil, and then only in certain regions, notably the Mediterranean, and North Africa. Most societies were based on relatively simple technologies, using limited amounts of energy, and with a limited territorial 'reach'. The exceptions, of course, numbered some of the world's great civilisations, but even in these cases (such as the Roman Empire and the empires of the Incas and Mayas in the Americas) sustainable production was often achieved for con-siderable periods of time. It took centuries for systems of raised-bed cultivation, or terracing, to reach the point at which they were no longer sustainable.

The Industrial Revolution in Europe changed this. After the eighteenth century, large-scale exploitation of fossil fuels enabled human societies to transform natural resources, by harnessing new forms of energy, the potential of which seemed limitless. The development of these 'hydrocarbon societies' not only revolutionised the use of energy, it stimulated new forms of trade throughout the globe. European commerce sought links with the colonies which were based on a new international division of labour. Instead of seeking precious metals and spices, the colonies were viewed as suppliers of raw materials for European industry and, later, as markets for European goods. As we shall see in the next chapter, the re-emergence of China as a significant manufacturer today needs to be viewed against a broad, historical backcloth. Before the eighteenth century most of the world's manufacturing was undertaken in Asia, particularly in China.

The Industrial Revolution was a revolution in the way energy was used, and goods produced. It stimulated free trade and led to the development of markets, and sourcing for those markets, from within vast territorial empires. It also led to serious environmental problems. Most of our environmental problems today have a global dimension, precisely because of the process of development initiated by the Industrial Revolution. Global capitalism and industrialisation prompted secondary, even tertiary, impacts on environments far removed from Western Europe or the United States. In its most recent phase advanced industrialisation has caused the following:

- concentration of greenhouse gases in the atmosphere;
- destruction of the ozone layer in the stratosphere;
- acidification of soils and surface water;
- build-up of toxic metals in sediments and soils;
- increasing radioactive wastes;
- accumulation of non-biodegradable chemicals;
- contamination and exhaustion of ground-water;
- loss of tropical forests and wetlands, together with their rich biodiversity.

These represent the major environmental problems that we face today, and any attempt to solve them has to acknowledge that they are global in scale. As Robert Ayres puts it, 'industrialization . . . is a process of uncontrolled, unsustainable "growth" that eventually destroys its host, the biosphere', (Ayres, in Ayres and Simonis 1994, xii).

THE LAWS OF THERMODYNAMICS

The principle that underwrites our planet is contained in the first two Laws of Thermodynamics. The First Law states that matter and energy are constant: they can neither be created nor destroyed. However, according to the Second Law of Thermodynamics, the quality of energy does change. The heat of a closed system diffuses to reach a uniform temperature. The extent of such uniformity is called entropy. Entropy increases until the closed system approaches absolute zero, the temperature at which all processes, and time itself, come to a halt. The uniformity of a closed system is equivalent to the disorder of its components. So, entropy is also a measure of disorder. As entropy increases within closed systems, so they become progressively disordered. A lump of coal contains concentrated hydrocarbons. It has a structure, it is ordered. The chemical bonds within the hydrocarbons represent free energy, which can be turned into mechanical and heat energy. After combustion, the ash, the heat and the carbon dioxide become dispersed and disordered.

The first two Laws of Thermodynamics suggest that the materials extracted from the natural environment for the production of goods and services must eventually be returned to the environment in degraded form. We cannot 'lose' matter, except in the form of energy. Ultimately all matter that is obtained from the Earth must be returned to it. This is, as Ayres notes, 'so simple a principle, but (carries) such profound implications' (Ayres 1994, xiii). Among the important issues with which this book is concerned are several which take us back to this axiom. Increasingly, we need to conserve the environment, especially in globally sensitive areas, because it acts as a sink for the waste materials (particularly carbon dioxide) that we generate from our use of matter.

At the same time, our limited understanding of the links between the conversion of matter, and its environmental consequences, should lead us to take precautionary measures. Such measures, in turn, might take us into a new form of relationship with nature, unlike that which dictated economic development in the past. For the countries of the South, whose vast populations and (generally) improved living standards pose an additional challenge, the question is whether they can 'leap-frog' over us, achieving the fruits of development, but on a truly sustainable basis.

Industrial systems are distinguished from those of nature in one important way. Natural systems are closed systems. That is, there are no external sources or sinks to such systems: they function by recycling nutrients, with the help of solar energy. Industrial systems, on the other hand, are open systems. In such systems, wastes are returned to nature in degraded form, principally pollution. There is no significant recycling of wastes from industrial systems, as we understand them today, and efforts to provide such recycling are in their infancy. It follows that industrial systems as presently constituted are, ultimately, unsustainable. The question is not whether questions of sustainability arise, but when and how.

What we recognise as biological evolution, in which humans play an important part, is a response to inherently unstable situations. Evolution has enabled new processes (organisms) to be invented, which stabilise the system, closing the circle and offering renewal. James Lovelock gave the word 'Gaia' to these immensely sensitive, naturally occurring processes.

These processes are themselves placed in jeopardy by human actions. The development of industrial systems has drastically shortened the timescale in which changes occur. In the past, economic development has been based on the natural availability of materials and resources, assisted by the development of new technologies of extraction. The propensity of industrial systems to recycle and re-use waste has not been a feature of the success of such systems. Wastes must, following the Laws of Thermodynamics, either be recycled, re-used, or dissipated into the environment.

Our industrial systems place little emphasis on either re-use or recycling, and the quantity of wastes increases as a consequence. Environmental management has sought to dilute or divert the stream of wastes we produce, from one medium (such as water, or land) to another (such as the air). However, our industrial systems, and the economic norms which drive them, are more concerned with the production of waste than with its destination.

To some extent, industrial societies have proved successful at shifting the emission of waste from one medium to another, but they have paid little attention to the ways that materials are metabolised. In most cases, environmental policy has served to dilute the waste-stream without materially affecting its volume. We have built sewage outlets that go further into the sea, and discharged gases from higher chimney stacks. We have substituted relatively benign materials for dangerous pollutants, like CFCs in aerosols. But we have scarcely begun to design our products, or our overall patterns of consumption, with their final destination in mind. We need to recover wastes and extend our control over the process of consumption itself.

The argument of this book is that if we fail to rise to this challenge, our ability to develop innovative new ways of managing the environmental contradictions of development can only serve to postpone our final denouement.

THE EFFECT OF HUMAN EVOLUTION ON NATURAL SYSTEMS

From the point of view of the physical sciences, sinks represent the location in which wastes interact with, and transform, ecosystems. These transformations would be hard enough to describe if industrial pollution had simply been cast out on a pristine natural environment, unencumbered by human activity. To make things more complicated, nature itself has already undergone significant changes during the pre-industrial period, at the hands of human populations. The form and significance of these alterations deserves some consideration (Allmark 1994).

Human societies evolved together with natural systems. The rate at which they transformed nature to survive (their metabolism) was at a biological minimum (Fischer-Kowalski and Haberl 1993). The evolution of the human brain, and with it reasoning, set in motion several parallel developments. One was the ability of humans to transform the environment in ways that benefited them. An early example is the way humans used fire. It was used for warmth and protection during the night, for clearing forests, for breaking stone, and for hunting and cooking animals. This brought in its train important ecological effects, particularly an increase in grassland habitats and, later, the extinction of the animals which were initially hunted. It also gave rise to the succession of fire-resistant trees, notably eucalyptus (Goudie 1986).

Human evolution also involved the development of language and verbal communication, which enabled cultures themselves to evolve. The ability of human societies to transmit and accumulate information greatly enhanced their ability to manipulate the human environment. Cultural evolution effectively speeded up the evolution of the human species in ways that accelerated the impact of humans upon their environment.

At the same time the new-found ability to designate and describe objects, so crucial for the construction of knowledge, contributed to the perception of 'other' and 'self' – necessary categories for the development of consciousness and, ultimately, what we call 'science'. The formation of consciousness and cultural identity were intimately related to the way humans conceptualised the world around them. As human societies gained the power to change natural systems, they slowly learned to conceive of themselves as separate from their environment. The development of industrial society, and the prospect of exponential rates of growth, even convinced some that society was not dependent on the environment. During the nineteenth century in Europe the belief in progress caught most thinking people in its net, notably economic and social theorists like Marx and Engels. The economic dependence on hydrocarbons was matched by a Promethean spirit.

The development of agriculture represented a colonisation of natural systems (Fischer-Kowalski and Haberl 1993). This involved expanding the area of intervention and exerting ever-more control over the ecosystem. Human survival depended upon increasing manipulation of natural ecosystems. The production of more foodstuffs from matter permitted increases in human population densities and prompted urbanisation. Urbanisation, in turn, ensured that agriculture expanded.

The ability to intervene in the environment was continually enhanced by harnessing natural forms of energy. The gravitational potential of water was used to develop complex irrigation systems and water-mills. Ploughing and transport were accomplished through animal traction. Sailing boats used wind power to extend the physical colonisation of the planet, and for the transportation of goods. The creation of human capital to control or manage the environment – buildings, boats, carts, ploughs, irrigation systems – led in turn to increased requirements of energy.

The effects of human metabolism on nature seem to have provided a positive feedback mechanism essential to human evolution, in a cultural as well as biological sense. Every time that the ecological impact of a particular form of social production diminished productivity, which as we have seen it did over long periods, so the crisis that ensued gave rise to new forms of production, with higher rates of metabolism (Debeir 1991).

The encounter between human societies and the environment presents several contradictory processes. Cultural evolution enabled human societies to distance themselves conceptually from the environment. At the same time, human dependence on unsustainable development placed a larger burden on the environment. The flow of the critical photosynthetic cycles, namely those of carbon, nitrogen, sulphur and phosphorus, was dramatically altered by industrial processes. 'Natural' systems have become so transformed by human purposes, that they became purposive systems, designed for human use, rather than systems which co-evolved with human societies. As Norgaard has argued, leaving the analysis of sink functions to natural scientists is an effect of the positivist dualism which itself spurred human societies towards increasingly unsustainable practices (Norgaard 1993).

Economic growth, as we shall see, is more than an empirical phenomenon, which can be reduced to the value placed on it by those who benefit most from it. Economic growth is an ideology firmly rooted in industrial society. Our willingness to intervene in the environment, without sparing the consequences, has become almost an article of faith. The more we intervene, of course, the more we need to manage and regulate the consequences of that intervention. In the main, the management role has been delegated to, or assumed by, natural scientists. In effect, natural science has become involved in the defence of a socially constructed ideology. Examples abound of the way in which the commercial exploitation of science has altered its trajectory, lending credence to the view that distancing ourselves from technology has often served to legitimate science.

In rather less conspiratorial a sense, most research in the sciences is directed to solving discrete problems, which appear to arise spontaneously. As resources become scarce, for example, scientific research is undertaken to find substitutes and alternatives. This serves to reinforce the idea of 'technical fixes' as solutions to human problems, and to emphasise that the solution to these problems lies in the regulation and control of environmental consequences (their management). Just as resources are treated in isolation from each other, so are sinks. The tendency is to treat each sink, or each pollutant, as an isolated problem.

Each scientific problem which is resolved by human intervention, using fossil fuels and manufactured materials, is viewed as a triumph of management, and a contribution to economic good, when it also represents a future threat to sustainability. Having jettisoned the fear that resources themselves were limited, in the 1970s, we are today faced by the prospect that the means we have used to overcome resource scarcity, substitution and increased levels of industrial metabolism, contribute to the next generation of problems which are associated with global sinks.

SUSTAINABLE DEVELOPMENT

Sustainable development was defined by the Brundtland Commission in the following way:

> development that meets the needs of the present without compromising the ability of future generations to meet their own needs.
>
> (WCED 1987)

This definition has been brought into service in the absence of agreement about a process which almost everybody thinks is desirable. However, the simplicity of this approach obscures underlying complexities and contradictions. Before exploring whether we can establish indicators of sustainability, it is worth pausing to examine the apparent consensus that reigns over sustainable development.

First, following the Brundtland definition, it is clear that 'needs' themselves change, so it is unlikely (as the definition implies) that those of future generations will be the same as those of the present generation. The question then is, where does development come into the picture? Obviously development itself contributes to needs, helping to define them differently for each generation, and for different cultures.

This raises the second question, not covered by the definition, of how needs are defined in different cultures. Most of the 'consensus' surrounding sustainable development has involved a syllogism: sustainable development is necessary for all of us, but it may be defined differently in terms of each and every culture. This is superficially convenient, until we begin to ask how these different definitions match up. If in one society it is agreed that fresh air and open spaces are necessary before development can be sustainable, it will be increasingly difficult to marry this definition of needs with those of other societies seeking more material wealth, even at the cost of increased pollution. And how do we establish which course of action is more sustainable? Recourse to the view that societies must decide for themselves is not very helpful. (Who decides? On what basis are the decisions made?). At the same time, there are problems in ignoring culturally specific definitions in the interest of a more inclusive ontology.

There is also considerable confusion surrounding *what* is to be sustained. One of the reasons why there are so many contradictory approaches to sustainable development (although not the only reason) is that different people identify the objects of sustainability differently.

For those whose primary interest is in ecological systems and the conservation of natural resources, it is the natural-resource base which needs to be sustained. The key question that is usually posed is the following: how can development activities be designed which help to maintain ecological processes, such as soil fertility, the assimilation of wastes, and water and nutrient recycling? Another, related, issue is the conservation of genetic materials, both in themselves and (perhaps more importantly) as part of complex, and vulnerable systems of biodiversity. The natural-resource base needs to be conserved because of its intrinsic value.

There are other approaches. Some environmental economists argue that the natural stock of resources, or 'critical natural capital', needs to be given priority over the flows of income which depend upon it. They make the point that human-made capital cannot be an effective substitute for natural capital. If our objective is the sustainable yield of renewable resources, then sustainable development implies the management of these resources in the interest of the natural capital stock. This raises a number of issues which are both political and distributive: who owns and controls genetic materials, and manages the environment? At what point does the conservation of natural capital unnecessarily inhibit the sustainable flows of resources?

Second, according to what principles are the social institutions governing the use of resources organised? What systems of tenure dictate the ownership and management of the natural-resource base? What institutions do we bequeath, together with the environment, to future generations? Far from taking us away from issues of distributive politics and political economy, a concern with sustainable development inevitably raises such issues more forcefully than ever.

The question 'what is to be sustained?' can also be answered in another way. Some writers argue that it is present (or future) levels of production (or consumption) that need to be sustained. The argument is that the growth of global population will lead to increased demands on the environment, and our definition of sustainable development should incorporate this fact. At the same time, the consumption practices of individuals will change too. Given the choice, most people in India or China might want a television or an automobile of their own, like households in the industrialised North. (This issue is further discussed in Chapter Four.) What prevents them from acquiring one is their poverty, their inability to consume, and the relatively 'undeveloped' infrastructure of poor countries.

Is there anything inherently unsustainable in broadening the market for TV sets or cars? If the answer is 'yes', then those of us who possess these goods need to be clear about why we consume goods unavailable to others. Our response is usually that it is difficult, or even impossible, to function in our society without information or private motorised mobility. But, as we shall see in Chapter Seven, this is to evade the question of underlying social commitments. We define our needs in ways which effectively exclude others meeting theirs, and in the process increase the long-term risks for the sustainability of their livelihoods. Most importantly, however, the process through which enlarging our choices serves to reduce those of others is largely invisible to us.

SUSTAINABILITY INDICATORS

If we concentrate our attention on our own society, we can begin by identifying aspects of our management of the environment that are unsustainable. It is a short step to the development of sustainability indicators. The growth of interest in sustainability indicators has followed that of sustainable development. Again, the importance of the issue is matched by the difficulty in addressing it convincingly. There are numerous indicators of *un*sustainability, but it has proved much more difficult to find those for sustainability.

The reasons for these difficulties are not hard to find. Economics developed, historically, around the idea of scarcity. The role of technology was principally that of raising output from scarce resources. Among other benefits of economic growth was the political legitimacy it conferred, within a dynamic economy, on those who could successfully overcome the obstacles to more spending. Wealth was a good thing, in itself.

This proposition, which underlines the difficulty in reconciling development with sustainability, strikes at the legitimation of only one form of value within capitalist, industrial societies. Habermas expressed his criticism of this view forcefully, in the following way:

> can civilisation afford to surrender itself entirely to the ...
> driving force of just one of its subsystems – namely, the pull of
> a dynamic ... recursively closed, economic system which can
> only function and remain stable by taking all relevant inform-
> ation, translating it into, and processing it in, the language of
> economic value.
>
> (Habermas, 1990)

There is another dimension to the problem of consumption, which is relatively recent. This is the extent to which, at the end of the twentieth century, we need to refer to genuinely global processes. As Miller has argued, global consumption 'provides a new egalitarianism between subject and subject' as Central Africans wear suits, Indonesians and Brazilians produce soap operas, and branded commodities acquire general importance (Miller 1994, 3). The ethnography of consumption has the same referents, and the commodities consumed are, in some ways, great levellers (Brewer and Porter 1993).

However, difficulties also remain in the way we measure wealth. William Cobbett, the early nineteenth-century radical, pointed to these over one hundred and sixty years ago, in supporting the reduction of factory hours for children from twelve to ten hours a day, in the textile mills. Speaking in support of Lord Shaftesbury's bill, Cobbett said:

> it is interesting to learn that all of Britain's wealth, power and
> security ... lay not in her virility, nor in her agriculture, banking
> or merchandise, but ... in the labour of three hundred thousand

little girls in Lancashire. [If two hours of their daily work were
deducted] away goes the wealth, away goes the capital, away
go the resources, the power and the glory of England! (cited in
Morris 1991).

The question today, as in the 1830s, is 'what is it worth to measure
wealth in this way?' It is often assumed that increasing sustainability
jeopardises the creation of wealth, but unless we are clear about how
we measure wealth, it is difficult to assert that the creation of wealth
is necessary for improvements in the quality of life. (An axiom in the
1993 UK White Paper on Science, *Realising Our Potential* (OST, 1993)).
The creation of wealth, as a policy objective, tends to confine
environmental factors to the closet, enabling politicians to wring their
hands over the supposed high levels of unemployment that higher
environmental standards herald, or the dangers of interfering with
market forces which are assumed to work best when they are free
from government control.

Similarly, within the European Union, a recent White Paper on
Growth, Competitiveness and Employment places emphasis on
economic growth and increased employment intensity as vehicles for
economic recovery (Brussels 1993). The familiar argument is that we
need to increase both growth and employment, to generate the means
to deal with environmental problems, before sustainability can be
achieved. In practice, increased private consumption is seen as the
key policy lever. If we increase the consuming capability of the
household within the European Union, we can invest the benefits in
employment-creating activities such as child care, education, voca-
tional training, and better facilities for the old and handicapped.

There is a problem in this line of argument that is rarely exposed
by either Left or Right in the political spectrum. The social policy
agenda that is supposed to be the beneficiary of increased growth
carries environmental implications, both in the goods and services
to be provided in the social field, and the means of achieving them.
If we pursue the creation of needs, as a means of lifting overall
consumption, and enhancing current production, we are unlikely to
identify the needs which our economic system currently does *not*
meet. There is a considerable risk that we will create more casual
employment rather than more socially useful employment and, in the
process of raising personal consumption, place environmental
standards in greater, rather than less, jeopardy. This issue is taken
up in Chapter Eight.

The alternative path to follow is a very radical one. It means pursuing better environmental standards – in energy production and conservation, in more efficient transport, better air and water quality – as the first objectives of policy, rather than the supposed beneficiaries of more economic growth. At the moment the European Union is setting environmental targets around 'what we can afford', from the wealth created by unsustainable levels of production and consumption. The alternative is to make environmental targets the *instruments* for improving the quality of our lives. As Fleming (1994) has argued, we need to bring sustainability out of the environmental closet and start applying it to the economy at large.

We can appreciate the importance of making radical changes in underlying economic processes if we examine the role of sustainability indicators at the global level. The process of consultation which led to the conference at Rio de Janeiro in 1992 was discussed in Chapter Two. The 'goalposts' for sustainable development, as far as the United Kingdom is concerned, are given in Box 3.1.

Box 3.1 Goalposts for Sustainable Development

The Rio Commitment

Britain is committed at home to:

- change unsustainable patterns of production and consumption;
- promote effective policy integration and long-term sustainable sectoral policies in the fields of energy, transport, agriculture, industry, construction and natural resource management;
- draw up national plans and strategies for sustainable development with full participation of concerned groups and organisations in this process;
- give the lead in major reductions of greenhouse-gas emissions.

Abroad, Britain is committed to:

- accept special responsibility, along with other Northern countries, to promote similar perspectives, policies and practices worldwide, and to this end to offer increased, but unspecified, help to the South.
- recognise that developing countries can only work with us in addressing the problem of global warming if we are prepared to provide sufficient relevant assistance.

- adopt policies which adequately address not just global environment degradation but also, in parallel, global poverty and inequalities.
- promote sustainable development worldwide in ways which give far greater emphasis than in the past to promoting a 'bottom up' approach which involves local communities and greater local and (implicitly) national democracy.

Long-term policy

Domestic and international policy objectives which need to be pursued if sustainable development is taken seriously will include the following:

- the rate of use of renewable resources not to exceed their rate of regeneration;
- the rate of depletion of non-renewable resources not to exceed the rate of development of renewable substitutes;
- waste generation and pollution not to exceed the assimilative capacity of the environment;
- a national economy under which the throughput of materials and use of energy is greatly reduced;
- an international trading and financial system in which the more powerful countries avoid 'importing sustainability' at the expense of others, or in other ways damage developing countries' ability to pursue their own policies for national sustainable development;
- movement away from strongly individualist consumerist-centred aspirations and lifestyles to far greater emphasis on healthier, greener and more community-centred living.

Long-term domestic policy instruments

- Using taxes, prices and subsidies to change the price of activities that are non-sustainable relative to those which are sustainable. This involves pricing resources to reflect fully their long-term social and environmental costs.
- Shifting from personal or labour-based taxes to resource- and pollution-based taxes.
- Modifying production and consumption patterns to minimise the use of natural resources (including closed industrial production processes, recycling, re-use, etc).
- Matching structural change in the national economy, including running down 'unsustainable' sectors of production and trade.

In the wake of the UNCED meeting there has been widespread disappointment that the quality of national reporting to the Commission on Sustainable Development has been so poor. In an effort to improve the level of reporting, and to help refine indicators for measuring sustainability, the New Economics Foundation has pioneered work into pilot indicators of national performance (NEF 1994).

Agenda 21 suggested that more work needed to be undertaken on sustainability indicators, particularly by United Nations agencies and other international bodies. At its first full session, the Commission on Sustainable Development also indicated that it was interested in using indicators in the reporting process. If it did so, this would place it far in advance of any existing system of collating information from national governments.

The approach of the New Economics Foundation and the World Wide Fund for Nature has been to concentrate on developing 'pilot indicators' as a first, and urgent, step towards the much longer process of agreeing indicators for measuring overall sustainability. An important precedent for this activity is the work undertaken by the Organisation for Economic Cooperation and Development (OECD) in seeking to develop a set of core indicators for environmental performance. These core indicators are being piloted in a number of country studies. In essence they seek to measure three things: the pressures placed on the environment (such as pollutant emissions); the current condition of the environment (such as atmospheric concentrations of greenhouse gases); and the responses of society to these problems (such as expenditure on air-pollution abatement).

The set of key indicators developed by the New Economics Foundation and the World Wide Fund for Nature is shown in Box 3.2. This framework reflects the issues as presented in Agenda 21, focusing on areas of concern where agreement is high. These key indicators of environmental performance reflect the outcomes of policy decisions that have already been taken, over a range of issues. They describe either environmental, social and economic conditions, or the pressures to which the environment is subjected. This kind of indicator is already used widely, although rarely in conjunction with sustainability planning (Jacobs 1991). The advantage, however, is that data are already available on many of these indicators, and a degree of consensus exists as to their usefulness and limitations (NEF 1994).

Box 3.2 A few indicators of sustainable development

Sustainable development is a process and not a condition, and there are many different and legitimate ways to go about it. The 'indicators' listed below are not precise objectives or standards, but merely a few – out of many possible – trends that one might expect to find in a society moving toward sustainability.

The use of energy and materials

- Per capita resource consumption, for a given standard of living, is dropping.
- The proportion of non-renewable energy usage in primary production is diminishing, while renewable sources, such as solar or human energy, are increasing: and sectors using non-renewable forms of energy are investing significantly to develop and apply technologies that will use renewable forms.
- Passenger kilometres travelled by public transport are increasing in proportion to those travelled by private motorised transport.
- There is a progressive increase in both official incentives to use renewable energy and disincentives to use non-renewable forms.
- There is an increasingly free flow of technology, especially to poor countries.

Ecological processes and biological wealth

- Development activities seek to maintain ecological processes (soil fertility, waste assimilation and water and nutrient cycling) and not to exceed the capacity of these processes.
- Development increasingly depends upon and conserves a growing range of genetic material, not only the different species but the varieties within species.
- Renewable resources are increasingly used and harvested at rates within their capacity for renewal.
- More and more areas of high value for their irreplaceable environmental services are not only being set aside, but are being effectively managed, with secure funding.

Policy, economics and institutions

- Economies – especially those that depend upon high-volume natural resource use – are diversifying, especially towards high-value information and service industries.
- There are growing numbers of formal mechanisms to integrate environmental and development concerns, and to insert environ-

mental values in prevailing systems of economic policy, planning and accounting.

- More accurate and representative economic indicators are being introduced to measure sustainable development, so that the currently dominant concerns of consumption, savings, investment and government expenditures are increasingly joined by measures of natural resource productivity and scarcity.
- More methods are being introduced for valuing use by future generations, for comparing such use to today's needs and for making equitable trade-offs between generations.
- Flows of resources to and from a given country are increasingly stable and equitable, and do not result in severe net depletion of the national resource base.
- Both the incidence and the effects of 'boom and bust' are diminishing.
- There are both regulatory measures that ensure that resource limits are not exceeded, and enabling measures that encourage voluntary improvements in technology to make more sustainable use of resources within those limits.
- Environmental monitoring is regularly and effectively carried out, and both policies and operations are adjusted to suit.
- Military budgets are decreasing in relation to budgets for work to ensure environmental security and sustainable development.

Society and culture

- The notion of resource limits, and the need for sustainability in production and livelihood systems, is increasingly prevalent in a society's values, embodied in its constitutions and inherent in its education systems.
- The community is becoming more diverse in terms of skills and enterprises, and yet remains coherent as a community.
- There is a growing body of commonly held knowledge and available technology for maintaining a good quality of life through sustainable activities.
- There is a tendency towards full employment, good job security and household stability.
- Increasing numbers of people have access to land adequate for sustaining good nutrition and shelter for their families and/or adequate, reliable incomes to pay for these necessities.
- The costs and benefits of resource use and environmental conservation are more equitably distributed: consumers increasingly choose to pay for goods and services that are resource-efficient and minimize environment degradation.
- Conflicts over land and resource rights are diminishing.

- People who once relied upon unsustainable activities for their livelihood are being supported in their transition to sustainable activities.
- Development is increasing people's control over their lives, the range of choices open to them and the knowledge to make the right choices: it is compatible with the culture and values of the people affected by it, and contributes to community identity.

Source: Holmberg et al 1991

The central point that is often lost is that the usefulness of sustainability indicators is directly related to the policy context which they are used to address. Setting targets for policy implies changes not only in what is measured, or how it is measured, but also, what it is that we are seeking to achieve. Using core indicators does not, in itself, provide a basis for devising new policies. However, it can provide a basis for making policy choices, which is quite a different thing. As the NEF (1994) document argues, setting sustainability targets is inevitably a political exercise. It is obviously subject to technical limitations, and deficiencies of data. Nevertheless, the major problem in achieving sustainability targets is not their comparative lack of refinement, but the very difficult (and rarely consensual) political choices that lead to them being adopted. It is these political choices which need to incorporate 'sustainability', not merely the quantitative indices against which they are measured.

In the real world, governments, when pressed to consider environmental policy, tend to adopt modified versions of the more thoroughgoing, radical alternatives on offer. These modified policies represent the 'soft' dimensions of sustainability policy, as opposed to the 'harder' dimensions advocated by environmental campaigners and activist groups. The contrast is brought out in Box 3.3, which compares both approaches. It is clear that the soft dimensions of sustainability policy require shifts in the level of resources allocated to problems, combined with the establishment of higher environmental standards. The harder measures, on the other hand, strike at fundamental policy choices, such as the shift away from road transport, or attempts to build the uses to which energy is put into the level of energy generated, and to organise production around principles of waste minimisation.

Box 3.3 Examples of 'soft' and 'hard' dimensions of sustainability policies

'Soft' dimensions

Reducing slightly domestic and industrial waste streams, and switching between land-fill and incineration treatments

Investing in some fields of public transport, especially if technologically smart or fashionable (trams)

Reducing some air pollution, via shift of some industries abroad and some technical improvements

Reducing most obvious of water pollution problems, to certain standards

Reducing slightly the rate of land consumption, via urban and regional planning

Reducing the worst effects on key wildlife ecosystems, especially in famous scenic zones

'Hard' dimensions

Reducing drastically domestic and industrial waste streams

Reducing car use, with a large shift to public transport

Reducing overall water use

Cutting the rate of land urbanisation (or de-ruralisation) to zero or nearly zero

Protecting connected ecosystems and especially fragile ones (especially water-based)

Shifting from road freight to rail and water (or even reducing the rate of shift from rail to road)

Reducing mining and quarrying (especially aggregates), except by increased imports

Reducing air travel (passenger or freight)

Transforming dramatically processes of chemical industries

Source: Marshall 1994

These kind of exercises underline the way in which environmental management translates normative environmental goals, and political choices, into measures of performance. This implies at least three things: a willingness on the part of government to manage the transition towards increased sustainability; an ability to do so (probably expressed as a high degree of consensus); and, finally, the expression of environmental goals in quantitative terms. It would be a mistake to view quantification as an answer to essentially political problems, as we shall see. For example, if countries spend more on environmental protection, it is unclear whether this is because the environment is getting better or worse. Yet, in terms of environmental management, what is being measured is the level of intervention. It is also clear that the first two prerequisites for meaningful sustainability planning rely heavily for their success on taking political decision-making out of the sphere of the 'here and now' and placing it in that of 'there and in the future'. It is necessary to reach political agreement around sustainable objectives before measures of performance can be put to any use.

At this point it is worth sounding a cautionary note. Ecological awareness is not synonymous with only one ideological position, such as the kind of internationalist social democracy expressed by the Brundtland Commission. One government in Europe before the Second World War was a pioneer in what we call 'environmentalism' today. In the 1930s organic farms were established where herbal medicines were grown. In 1934 this government had already promoted nature reserves, and legislated to ensure that new tree plantations would include broad-leaved deciduous trees, as well as conifers. Hedgerows were protected by law, and animals were protected against vivisection. In 1941, during the War itself, a ban was placed on artificial fertilisers, on the grounds that they were 'unnatural'. All these measures, and others, were taken by the Nazi Government in Germany (Bramwell 1989). We might pause to contemplate the different social forces that drive ecological awareness before applauding its various manifestations with equal conviction. An interest in the environment may not be linked to humane social, and democratic, political objectives. We also need to consider the social cost of meeting environmental targets.

Chapter Four

The Global Economy and Consumption

In the last chapter we established that environmental targets imply social choices. Before we can fully appreciate the importance of a theory of metabolism which considers the role of human choices in transforming the environment, we need to understand the processes through which global political economy is itself being transformed. The industrialisation project, which has come to characterise the experience of the developed countries, has undergone profound changes since 1970. Increasingly the 'limits' placed on economic growth are not only those of resource-scarcity but of 'plenty', particularly in the form of hidden 'externalities' – air pollution, declining water quality, vulnerable ecosystems – which threaten to undermine the very economic systems from which they are derived. Although these changes often reflect material advances in the standard of living, they are, in turn, serving to undermine the quality of life. This chapter examines the relationship between the evolution of an industrial model based on hydrocarbons, which has itself fuelled increased global consumption, and the environmental costs of this model.

THE HYDROCARBON SOCIETY AND ENERGY CONSUMPTION

Before 1950, the annual rise in commercial energy consumption, at the global level, stood at just over 2 per cent. In the following decade, the figure more than doubled to almost 5 per cent. During the 1960s, the annual rise in commercial energy consumption exceeded 5.5 per cent. The rise in oil prices in the 1970s gave rise to more uncertainty about the availability of fossil fuel reserves, and there was a slow-down in energy consumption. The crisis surrounding hydrocarbons did not, however, seriously undermine their place in the process of industrialisation. Rather, it served to underline the fact that economic growth, fuelled by hydrocarbons, would need to advance along a trajectory marked by lower energy intensity.

The lower-energy transition was most marked in the shift away from coal, which in the 1920s accounted for almost 80 per cent of commercial energy consumption. The discovery of new oil reserves, and technological developments in the petrochemical industries, served to ensure more reliable supplies of oil and a vast expansion in the uses to which it was put. By the 1950s, a profound shift had occurred throughout the developed world towards both production processes, and consumer patterns, based squarely on the availability of cheap oil. This shift from coal to oil was essentially complete in most of the developed world by the 1970s, the decade in which the market value of commercial energy rose to prominence at the international level. Most of the advances in the industrialisation of the developing countries occurred after the oil shocks of the 1970s. (Figure 4.1 shows the structure of energy consumption per person in 1992, tracking the rise in oil and natural gas as components of primary energy consusmption since the turn of the twentieth century. Figure 4.2 plots the shifts in energy consumption per capita against the background of economic growth. It demonstrates vividly the transition, since about 1920, towards lower energy intensity. Figure 4.3 expresses this transition as a relationship between the rate of economic growth and the consumption of energy. Among the developed countries, New Zealand has a low rate of growth and a high level of energy consumption. Japan illustrates the opposite: high growth combined with relatively low levels of energy consumption.)

Between 1970 and 1990 there was a 62 per cent increase in global commercial energy consumption, an increase much lower than in the previous two decades (Tolba et al 1992). There were also important changes in the mix of hydrocarbons and other sources of energy. The share of oil decreased between 1970 and 1990 from almost one half

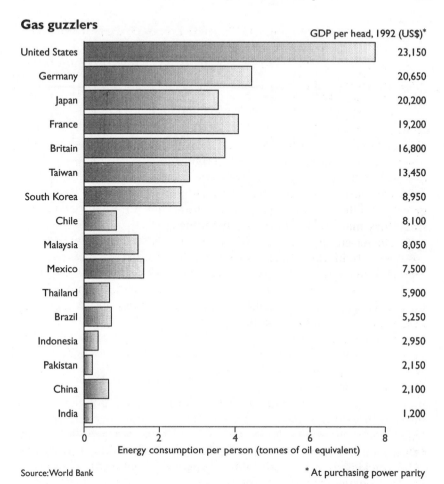

Figure 4.1 Energy consumption per person, selected countries, 1992

to just over one third of the total. At the same time the share of natural gas and coal increased by small amounts, and that of nuclear energy from 1.6 to 4.3 per cent.

The industrialised countries of the North account for the lion's share of commercial energy consumption. These industrial market economies, including the former Soviet Bloc states, account for almost 82 per cent of the commercial energy consumed, and account for about 22 per cent of the global population. The remaining 78 per cent of the world's population consume about 18 per cent of commercial energy, supplemented, in many cases, by locally available biomass materials, which are not traded. Perhaps the most revealing statistic

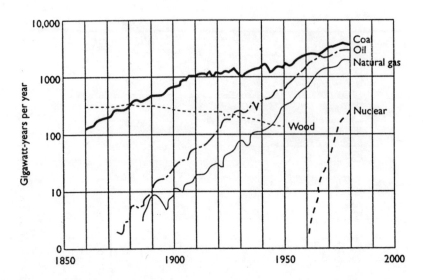

Source: Thomas H Lee, 'Advanced fossil systems and beyond', in Ausubel and Sladovich.

Figure 4.2 World primary energy consumption, 1850–1980

to lie behind the current crisis provoked by hydrocarbon use is that the developed world consumes about ten times the per capita energy of the countries in the South. (Figure 4.4 shows the proportions of commercial energy consumed by the developed and developing countries. Figure 4.5 shows total energy consumption by source, to 1990.)

In the developing countries, significant levels of commercial energy are consumed by a minority of the population, mainly resident in cities, and with high personal incomes. In the so-called 'informal' sector in cities, and in most of the countryside, household energy needs are met by fuelwood, agricultural residues and animal manure, as well as animal and human labour. This non-commercial sector is extremely important in assessing the consequences, as well as the responsibilities, of global changes such as enhancement of the Greenhouse Effect, and serves to underline the need to make connections between sources and sinks in arriving at more sustainable energy models.

It would be wrong to over-simplify the relationship between energy consumption and economic growth, since the structure of an

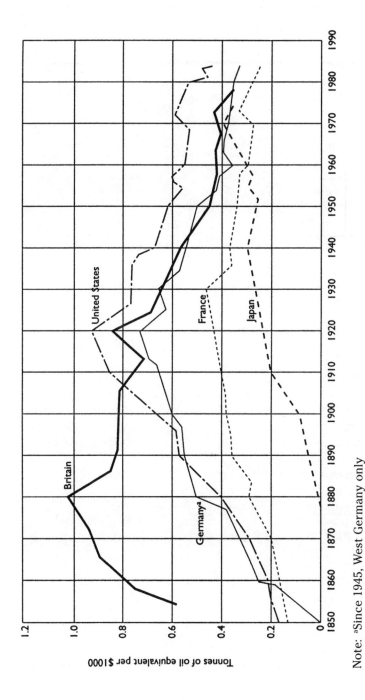

Figure 4.3 Primary energy consumption relative to real GDP, selected countries, 1850–1982

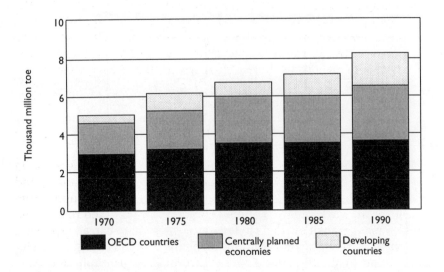

Source: El-Hinnawi 1991, in Tolba et al 1992

Figure 4.4 Total commercial energy consumption by region, 1970–1990

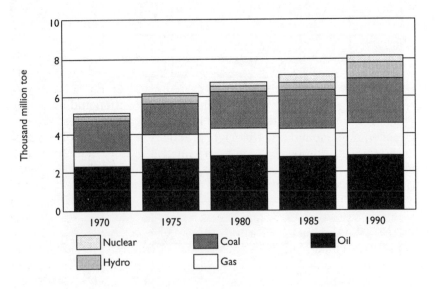

Source: El-Hinnawi 1991, in Tolba et al 1992

Figure 4.5 Total commercial energy consumption by source, 1970–1990

economy appears to be as important as its size in determining the energy options available. Countries dependent on energy-intensive exports demonstrate rates of economic growth linked to energy use. However, in the poorer countries dependent on primary exports, the rate of economic growth frequently exceeds that of energy use. In the more industrialised countries of the North, and increasingly many of the newly industrialising countries, steady improvements in the efficiency of energy conversion, and energy utilisation, have demonstrated that higher levels of growth can be achieved with lower per capita levels of energy consumption.

Developed, and developing, countries are increasingly differentiated on the basis of the lifestyles of their inhabitants. The way houses and offices are heated and illuminated, the amount of commuting from suburbs, to work and to shopping complexes, decreased reliance on urban mass transit systems in favour of the private car, all represent features of everyday consumption which affect the energy intensity transition. While the gross national product, in per capita terms, is similar in the United States and in Japan, it is remarkable that per capita energy consumption in Japan is half that of the United States. In Chapters Five and Six it is argued that these issues surrounding personal mobility and lifestyle need to be placed within the global context, as prerequisites for workable international agreements, and in tracing the lines of responsibility for global environmental problems.

As we shall see, one of the major challenges to global energy consumption arises from the way in which the energy intensity transition is effected in the developing countries. For a variety of reasons, measures to encourage energy conservation and improved efficiency have been rather limited in developing countries. The use of old equipment and technological practices in the South often leads to energy consumption which is very much higher than in the North. In many countries the use of quotas for industrial production means that there is little or no incentive to reduce energy consumption. These problems have been exacerbated by poor maintenance of facilities, the subsidisation of energy prices to consumers (including industry) and poor monitoring of consumption, as well as losses in energy transmission. The substitution of commercial over non-commercial sources of energy, a token of urbanisation, has not brought about a corresponding increase in economic growth, in many cases. In effect, traditional sources of energy constituted an invisible subsidy to the development process which, once removed, implies a cost against lowered energy intensity.

Before exploring the shifts in lifestyle associated with increased consumption, we need to examine the main developments in the industrial sectors of both developed and developing countries, which have generated changes in consumption.

In 1990 it was estimated that the total 'value added' by global manufactures had increased from $US2500 billion (1975) to a little under $4000 billion, at constant 1980 prices (Tolba et al 1992, 323). This represents the difference between the value of industrial products and the cost of the inputs that go into producing them. It does not, however, reflect the full environmental costs of industrial production: suggesting that market 'values' are a poor indicator of the costs implied throughout the life cycle of a product. This is particularly true for developing countries whose natural resources play a large part in the finished product (such as petroleum refining and mining activities) or where labour costs are important in processing natural resources (such as tanning and textiles). Most developing countries have yet to make significant encroachments into high-tech, knowledge-intensive industries such as microelectronics, information technology and biotechnology. These are the areas in which the developed countries have made the biggest strides. In the industrialised countries, the growth in these industries has been more than double that of the traditional sectors, such as iron and steel production and petroleum refining.

The environmental impacts of industrialisation depend upon the type and scale of the industrial activity, as well as the physical environment of different regions. Following the United Nations Environment Programme, it is possible to distinguish three different categories of environmental impact: those brought about by new high-tech industries in the industrialised economies; impacts in the newly industrialising economies and oil-exporting countries; and those affecting poorer countries with vulnerable ecosystems and population pressures on natural resources.

The changes in economic activity at the global level are reflected in shifts in world trade. Since the 1960s, the exports from developing countries have shifted away from primary materials, agricultural products and foodstuffs towards increasing exports of manufactured goods (see Figure 4.6, *The commodity structure of world trade*). Some of these manufactures utilise new technological processes and materials. Many of the new technologies are less material- and energy-intensive. However, such technologies are also heavy users of complex, new, toxic materials that produce contaminants such as heavy metals, toxic gases, water pollutants and hazardous wastes.

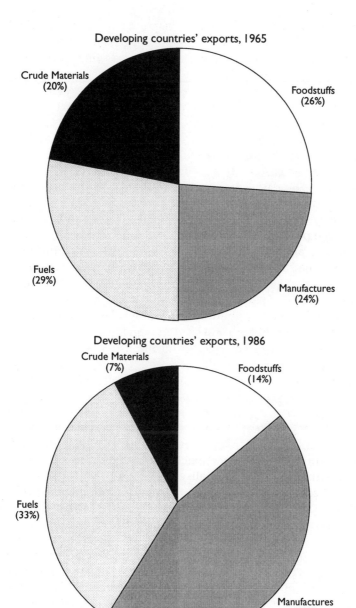

Figure 4.6 Commodity structure of world trade, 1965 and 1986

The full environmental impact of these production technologies is difficult to ascertain. The same observation holds for the new biotechnologies that are set to transform the agricultural and pharmaceutical industries.

The outline of industrial metabolism in the previous chapter demonstrated how the impact of industrial activities extends over the entire chain of events, from raw material extraction, through the manufacturing process itself, to the disposal of wastes. In addition, many industrial products themselves become hazardous when they are disposed of carelessly. Like the processes with which they are associated, they carry risks which are not quantified or added into the environmental equation.

The 'hydrocarbon society', which emphasises relentless industrialisation, places heavy demands on the consumption of non-renewable resources. Although the total share of energy consumption attributable to industry declined between 1970 and 1987, most notably in Japan, there were worrying developments in the sources of hydrocarbons used. India, China and South Africa, in particular, represent economies whose combined populations are a significant proportion of the global total, and in which industrialisation is still dependent on coal-burning, with all the associated environmental consequences.

Industrialisation has also increased the demand for non-renewable mineral resources, particularly iron-ores, and consequently increased the drive to recover metals and recycle wastes. However, the advantages consequent upon the declining relative importance of certain minerals have been more than offset by the dangers inherent in global production of plastics. As the Organisation for Economic Cooperation and Development (OECD) has shown, plastics have replaced almost 10 per cent of natural materials in some industrial sectors (OECD 1991) and this share is expected to rise dramatically.

The primary role of industry in generating demand for commercial energy is still evident in data from developing countries. As a recent World Bank study of market demand for commercial energy in seven developing countries (Brazil, China, Indonesia, Malaysia, Pakistan, Philippines and Thailand) concluded, by 2010 industry will have increased its share of energy consumption from 51 per cent to 56 per cent (IBRD 1990). One implication of this growth is that opportunities for energy conservation in the industrial sector of developing countries will grow in the future. As an example, energy consumption in the Indian iron and steel industry could be reduced by 12 per cent, if capacity was better utilised. Similar gains could be made in other developing countries, such as Thailand and Egypt (Tolba et al 1992). Together with gains in recovering waste materials, and reducing the harmful social and environmental effects of waste, energy conservation measures represent a significant challenge for North/South economic and political relations in the future. These issues receive attention later in this chapter.

A significant part of the increase in energy consumption, at the global level, is attributable to increased population. Table 4.1 provides an estimate of the share of increased energy consumption due to population and improved living standards by continent. It also gives figures for per capita energy consumption between 1960 and 1981. It is clear that the largest increases, in percentage terms, occurred in Europe, where population increase was less significant than improvements in living standards.

Table 4.1 Population growth and energy consumption, 1960–1981

Region	Percentage of increased energy consumption due to			Energy consumption per capita*	
	Population	Living standards		1960	1981
World	46	54		38	55
Africa	33	67		6	12
N America	51	49	USA	236	281
			Canada	164	286
S America	37	63		16	28
Asia	18	82		8	20
Europe	16	84		72	124

Note: * 10^9 joules per person

Source: computed from data in United Nations Environment Programme *Environmental Data Report*, Blackwell, Oxford, 1987

Nevertheless, in Africa for example, improved living standards served to influence aggregate consumption, but by 1984 per capita consumption was only a fraction (less than one-twentieth) of consumption in North America. Increases in industrial activity, as well as population, in Asia, since 1984, which are outlined in the next section, are likely to put increasing pressure on the environment, from the standpoints of both increased energy consumption and the disposal of wastes.

THE NEW INTERNATIONAL ECONOMIC ORDER

The most important environmental aspect of the international division of labour is the effect of poverty, within even the middle-income countries which have experienced partial industrialisation. In the poorest countries, including most of Africa, and much of South Asia, increased dependence on an impoverished environment has reduced carrying capacity and undermined any serious attempts at increasing sustainability. Since the early 1980s a succession of structural adjustment policies, on the top of growing external indebtedness, have served to exacerbate many of the attempts being made to overcome poverty in the South. Commodity prices have fallen dramatically in value, in real terms, since the early 1980s, while debt repayment has increased. In some of the poorest countries – severely indebted low-income economies – such as those of Africa, external debt almost equals gross national product, and approaches four times the value of total exports, a fourfold increase in under a decade (UNEP 1994).

The combined effect of servicing debts, and reducing aid, is a net financial flow from the South to the North. In 1989, the developing countries paid $US59 billion in interest on their debts, and received official development assistance of $34 billion. In the same year the official debt of low- and middle-income countries grew by an average of 4 per cent. The only way out of this impasse, of course, has been for the developing countries to meet their spiralling debt burdens by continually increasing their exports. The extraordinary fact is that so many of them have been able to do so – although not without impact on their, often fragile, environments.

The economic hegemony of the developed world can be judged from the 'eggtimer' diagram (Figure 4.7) below. This shows that, if we break global income down into five quintiles, almost all the tradeable economic activity is confined to the richest 20 per cent of countries. These countries (the North) represent nearly 83 per cent of income; 81 per cent of world trade; 95 per cent of commercial lending; and over 80 per cent of both domestic saving and domestic investment. The poorest quintile represents only about 1 per cent of all these activities.

These global inequalities do not imply that developing countries are less integrated into the world economy: rather, their trade with the North is growing in ways that are of increasing importance to their more developed neighbours. In 1992, 42 per cent of US exports were to developing countries, as were 48 per cent of Japan's. The

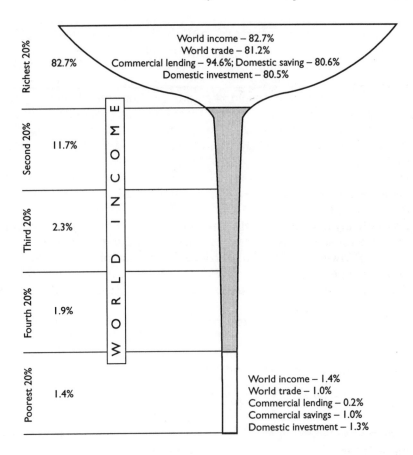

Figure 4.7 Global income and economic disparities (1992)

developing world accounted for only 20 per cent of the exports of the European Union in the same year. However, economic integration through trade reflects different forms of global interdependence.

It is important to remember the changing context of North/South economic relations. First, the last thirty years has seen a major shift in the commodity structure of world trade. Developing countries can no longer be characterised as primary producers, if judged by their export earnings. Figure 4.6 shows how the commodity structure of world trade changed between 1965 and 1986. Foodstuffs and raw materials (excluding fossil fuels) made up almost one half of the developing countries' exports in 1965. Twenty years later this had shrunk to barely 20 per cent of export values. In the same period, manufactured exports increased from just under one quarter to almost one half of all exports by value. In the decade since 1986 this process has been intensified and, as we shall see, carries important repercussions for the patterns of consumption in the South (as well as the North).

Economic growth in developing countries has been concentrated in a few areas, which have either been forcibly restructured, like much of Latin America since 1982, or have developed competitive market economies, some of which represent a threat to the economic dominance of some developed countries. Table 4.2 uses World Bank statistics to show the projected growth in gross domestic product (GDP) in real terms, by major world regions. It can be observed that, according to these projections, while economic growth in the North will remain more or less static during the next twenty years, the developing countries are likely to increase their rate of economic growth by over 50 per cent, from an annual average of 3 per cent, to one of 4.8 per cent.

A closer look at this picture, however, reveals large imbalances

Table 4.2 Real GDP growth, North and South, annual average (%)

	1974–1993	1994–2003
Rich industrialised countries	2.9	2.7
Developing countries of which:	3.0	4.8
East Asia	7.5	7.6
South Asia	4.8	5.3
Latin America	2.6	3.4
East Europe and former Soviet Union	1.0	2.7
Sub-Saharan Africa	2.0	3.9
Middle East and North Africa	1.2	3.8

Source: World Bank 1994

within the category of developing countries itself. The economies of East Asia, and to a lesser extent South Asia, are likely to experience annual average increases in GDP of between 5 and 8 per cent during the next two decades. Since the populations of Asia are so large, and growing so rapidly, what might appear to be relatively modest levels of growth imply enormous increases in levels of personal and collective consumption and, ultimately, of course, equally large increases in the throughput of goods and services. (See Figure 4.8, *Where people will be in 2020*).

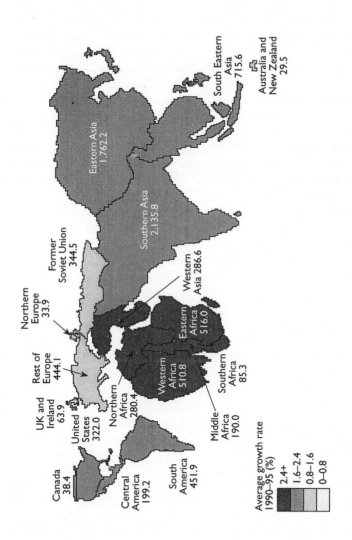

Figure 4.8 Where people will be in 2025 (projected population, in millions)

Figure 4.9 extrapolates future trends in economic growth from current indicators. It uses 'purchasing power parity' rather than US dollar equivalents, to provide a picture of the size of the world's largest economies in 2020. It does so because the purchasing power of money varies enormously between countries; dollar equivalents do not reflect the real value of goods and services. Figure 4.9 suggests that although in 1992 the United States was much the largest economy in the world, more than twice as big as its competitors in Japan and China, by 2020 China's economy will be 40 per cent bigger than that of the United States. Perhaps more significantly, however, China's average income could rise (at 6–7 per cent growth in GDP per head) to $13,000 (US) if measured by purchasing power parity. This is roughly the value for Spain today. At the same time, other Asian economies, like Korea and Indonesia, will be bigger in aggregate than most European economies, and the purchasing power of their populations will also be rising.

These figures are projections, and it can be argued that a high degree of uncertainty should be attached to them. The governing assumptions are that Asian economies continue to grow at 6 per cent per annum, and that their distribution of incomes remains the same. At the same time, we cannot afford to ignore the implications of these figures for wider patterns of trade and consumption. First, the proportion of Asia's exports going to other Asian countries (excluding Japan) rose from 26 per cent in 1986 to 37 per cent in 1992. Furthermore, unlike the existing Asian 'Tigers' (Singapore, South Korea, Hong Kong, Taiwan) the other newly industrialising countries in Asia are likely to encourage imports and unlikely to accumulate trade surpluses.

The effects of these economic patterns on consumption will be marked. Many Asian countries, such as India and China, represent a vast market for goods from Europe and North America; *The Economist* estimated 700 million 'new' consumers coming onto the world market, mainly from China, Indonesia and India, out of total populations of approximately three billion (*The Economist*, 1994a). This is roughly equal to the combined population of North America, the European Union and Japan in 1992. These new consumers will increasingly require not only more goods, but more energy in their use, and in their production. Refrigerators, televisions and automobiles absorb energy in their production, as well as in their use.

The demand for energy can also be expected to stimulate the demand for more durable consumer goods, particularly air conditioners (in semi-tropical climates) and refrigerators. Since 1978 the

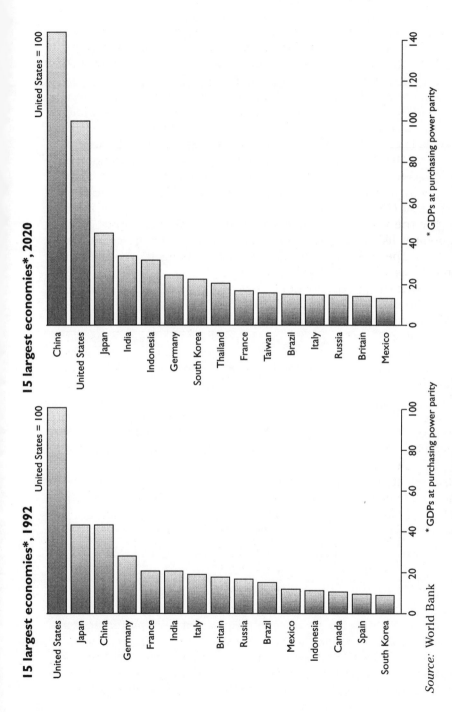

Figure 4.9 The world's 15 largest economies, 1992 and 2020

number of electric fans in China has increased twenty-fold, and the number of washing machines has risen from almost none to approximately 97 million appliances. (Table 4.3 shows the growth rates in world electricity consumption. Figure 4.10 shows the increase in China's electricity generation capacity to the year 2000.) Only 67 per cent of households in China were connected to the mains electricity supply by 1992, which was low even by Asian standards (82 per cent of Indian homes are on the grid). Further industrialisation serves to increase the demand for energy. In 1993, China boosted investment in its power industry by one fifth, to about $8.7 billion (US). In the same year China's oil consumption leapt by 11 per cent, turning the world's sixth biggest oil producer into an oil importer for the first time since the early 1970s. To cope with increased energy demand, it has been calculated that China must increase generating capacity by more than 20,000 MW each year, which far exceeds installed capacity.

Table 4.3 Growth rates of world electricity consumption, 1971–1989

	Compound growth rates (per cent per year)		
	1971–1980	**1980–1989**	**1971–1989**
1 Africa	11.1	3.6	7.3
2 Latin America	9.2	5.7	7.4
3 Asia	9.1	8.5	8.8
4 China	9.0	7.9	8.5
5 Middle East	14.8	9.9	12.3
6 TWCs	9.6	7.3	8.5
7 OECD	4.3	2.7	3.5
8 World	5.2	3.6	4.4

Note: item 6 is the sum of items 1–5; item 1 excludes S. Africa.

Source: calculated from IEA (International Energy Agency) 1991, *Energy Statistics and Balances of Non-OECD Countries 1988–89*, ORCD, Paris, 172–174

Some of China's energy consumption is not only profligate, but linked to existing technologies that do not use energy efficiently. Currently China uses 35 per cent more energy per tonne in steel production than the United States. While energy prices remain relatively low they discourage efficiency in production, conservation

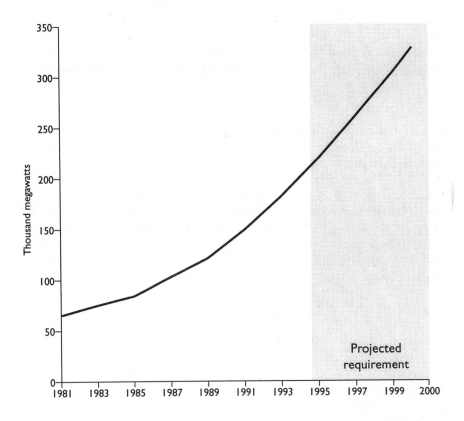

Figure 4.10 China's electricity generation capacity, 1981–2000

and end uses. China has the largest coal reserves in the world, but they are a long way from the point of greatest demand. Another option is to emphasise hydropower, whose potential is only beginning to be realised. However, plans like the Three Gorges dam across the Yangtze, which has been dreamed of for many years, will carry enormous environmental consequences and involve the removal of more than one million people from their homes.

ENERGY CONSUMPTION AND THE GENERATION OF WASTE

The generation of commercial energy raises a number of important issues about potential conflicts and complementarities between environment and development. We have largely been concerned with the contribution of economic growth, and population increase, to the generation of power and the consumption of goods and services. However, energy demand is also linked to the environmental issues discussed in earlier chapters: increasing levels of pollution and the production of waste.

The World Bank has estimated that electricity demand in the developing countries is expected to grow at an average rate of 6.6 per cent a year during the 1990s, raising the total amount of installed generating capacity by more than 80 per cent in one decade (Pearson 1995). Coal is expected to provide almost one half of the increased supply of electricity, and hydropower another third. As we have seen, the contribution of coal to economic growth in the South is a factor of enormous importance for the global environment. Coal's contribution to developing-country electricity supply is expected to double in volume during the 1990s. This carries implications not only for global climate change, but for air pollution in specific localities.

Several areas of environmental concern are closely linked with increasing energy generation in the South:

- major environmental accidents and risks;
- water pollution;
- land-use disturbance;
- radiation and radioactivity;
- the disposal of solid wastes;
- hazardous air pollution;
- acid deposition; and
- anthropogenic climate change.

As Pearson notes, unless there is much wider use of pollution-abatement technologies, it is probable that the emission of greenhouse gases from developing countries will increase fourfold between 1990 and 2010, and tenfold between 1990 and 2030. (Pearson 1995)

The recognition that generating more energy, driven by higher levels of consumption, will pollute the environment, constitutes only the first part of the problem. For developing countries there often appears to be a trade-off between expenditure on energy generation, and the allocation of funds to deal with some of its consequences – notably, environmental problems. This is another example of the way in which, in the absence of sustainable policies, scarce capital is diverted towards the consequences of pollution, rather than its causes.

Advocates of a 'no regrets' policy argue that measures to enhance energy efficiency also yield environmental benefits in the longer term, while improving energy efficiency in the short term (Grubb 1991). However, the key to improving both energy efficiency and many aspects of the environment, is the degree to which reducing the price of energy will lead to its increased consumption. There is enormous potential, in the South as well as the North, for fiscal policies which reduce pollution, and pricing arrangements which enable less energy to be generated for the same effect. Raising the economic efficiency of energy production might 'liberate substantial public and private resources that could be allocated to other environmental services, such as water supply, sanitation and health' (Pearson 1995, 5).

The trade-offs between consumption forgone, and future environmental benefits which are difficult to calculate, leaves most developing countries in a quandary. They do not wish to jeopardise their economic development, and the standard of living of their populations, particularly those who have not joined the electric grid. They also feel, with justice, that the industrialised countries want them to accept the trade-offs which are in the interests of those countries. This cannot be resolved until both developed and developing countries re-negotiate their economic inter-dependence, and develop a formula for compensating countries in the throes of rapid economic development. Experience with the Montreal Protocol, the international agreement which limits various ozone-destroying chemicals, has not been particularly propitious. *The Economist* recently reported that of the $393 million (US) pledged by the industrialised world for the transfer of technologies to the South between 1991 and 1994, only $216 million had been received (*The Economist*, 1994b). India's environment minister, Kamal Nath, expressed concern that this poor disbursement record would make donors much less likely to stump up the $510 million deemed necessary for the next three-year programme under the Montreal Protocol.

As we have seen, there is little sign that a global compact to effectively halt greenhouse gas emissions will emerge in the wake of the Earth Summit. The problems associated with such emissions do not rest upon substitute technologies, the use of which has already been anticipated by a few leading multinational companies, as is the case with CFCs.

RECOVERING CONSUMPTION: THE POLITICAL ECONOMY OF WASTES

Pollution accompanies economic growth. In the developed, industrialised countries, the management of waste and pollution is a problem of growing proportions. As Table 4.4 indicates, the volume of municipal wastes in the countries of the North is growing annually, a growth that is matched by that for industrial wastes. In the late 1980s the volume of industrial waste in most of the countries of Western Europe was roughly three times that for household waste (OECD 1991; Tolba 1992, 346). Each person in these countries was responsible for the annual generation of between three and four hundred kilograms of municipal waste. Although the proportion of industrial waste that was classified as 'hazardous' was relatively low (less than one fifth of all industrial waste) the total of hazardous waste in the OECD countries was over 303 billion tonnes in 1990.

Disposing of waste constitutes a major environmental problem. Of the main routes for disposal – incineration, composting, land fill and

Table 4.4 Quantities of municipal waste generated, by country, 1980 and 1990 (kg/inhabitant)

Country	1980	1990
Austria	222[6]	320
Belgium[2]	313	343
Canada	524	601
France	260	328
Germany	348[1]	318[4]
Greece	259	296
Italy	249	348
Japan	355	408
Luxembourg	351	448
Netherlands	489[5]	497
Norway	416	472
Portugal	214	287
Spain	270[7]	322[3]
Sweden	302	374
Switzerland	351	441
UK	319	398
USA	723	803

[1] Situation before 3/10/90; [2] 1989; [3] 1988; [4] 1987; [5] 1982; [6] 1979; [7] 1978

Source: Eurostat

recycling/re-use – most of the major industrialised countries have come to depend upon land-fill, as Table 4.5 shows. Land-fill is fraught with dangers, particularly as the disposal of chemical products increases. Between 1990 and 2005, the number of chemical products being disposed of through the normal waste disposal channels is expected to double. Recycling represents an avenue in which potential savings are enormous: in the energy and water used in the production of goods, which can be recovered, and in the reduced effects of water and air pollution discharges and emissions (UNEP 1991). In addition, of course, land-fill requires land, which is in short supply near many large conurbations.

Pollution is not only generated by disposing of products; it is also the result of much higher levels of personal mobility. As urban densities grow and more people travel further to work, the private car assumes more, rather than less, importance, in personal com-

Table 4.5 Waste disposal routes, by country (expressed as percentage by weight of municipal solid waste (MSW)

Country	Amount (ktonnes/yr)	Combustion	Landfill	Composting	Recycling
Austria	2,800	11	65	18	6
Belgium	3,500	54	43	0	3
Canada	16,000	8	80	2	10
Denmark	2,600	48	29	4	19
Finland	2,500	2	83	0	15
France	20,000	42	45	10	3
Germany	25,000	36	46	2	16
Greece	3,150	0	100	0	0
Ireland	1,100	0	97	0	3
Italy	17,500	16	74	7	3
Japan	50,000	75	20	5	–*
Luxembourg	180	75	22	1	2
Netherlands	7,700	35	45	5	16
Norway	2,000	22	67	5	7
Portugal	2,650	0	85	15	0
Spain	13,300	6	65	17	13
Sweden	3,200	47	34	3	16
Switzerland	3,700	59	12	7	22
UK	30,000	8	90	0	2
USA	177,500	16	67	2	15

Sources: TNO, OECD, IWM (some figures have been rounded up)

MSW: * MSW levels in Japan are calculated after the removal of recyclables

muting. Table 4.6 compares cities in terms of their urban density and the percentage of workers using private cars and public transport to travel to their place of work. As densities grow, public transport assumes more importance, but nevertheless even in European cities like Stockholm, Munich and Vienna, well over a third of commuters travel to work by car. Less than half of all commuters use public transport in these cities.

Table 4.6 Urban densities and commuting choices in selected cities

| City | Land use intensity (pop + jobs/ha) | Percentage of workers using | | |
		Private car	Public transport	Walking/ cycling
Phoenix	13	93	3	3
Perth	15	84	12	4
Washington	21	81	14	5
Sydney	25	65	30	5
Toronto	59	63	31	6
Hamburg	66	44	41	15
Amsterdam	74	58	14	28
Stockholm	85	34	46	20
Munich	91	38	42	20
Vienna	111	40	45	15
Tokyo	171	16	59	25
Hong Kong	403	3	62	35

Source: Lowe 1991

The growth in ownership of private cars, particularly in some Asian countries, and the increased reliance on roads to transport freight in the transitional economies of Central and Eastern Europe, suggest that levels of urban pollution associated with motor vehicles will continue to rise, together with urban congestion. Figures 4.11a and 4.11b show the growth in the world automobile fleet, between 1950 and 1990, and the corresponding fall in the number of people travelling in each vehicle (United Kingdom Environmental Foresight Project 1993, 82).

These trends are exacerbated by increasing numbers of journeys undertaken for tourist reasons: between 1972 and 1990, their number rose by 240 per cent, to 438 million individual journeys undertaken by tourists (Tolba et al 1992).

According to the World Bank (*The Economist* 1994), countries celebrated for rapid economic growth, such as some of the economies

a) World automobile fleet

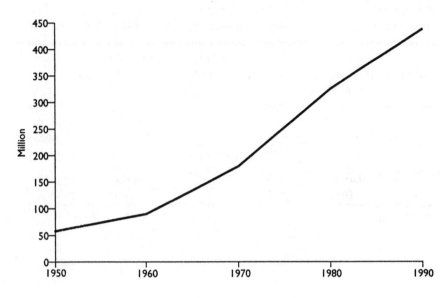

b) People per automobile

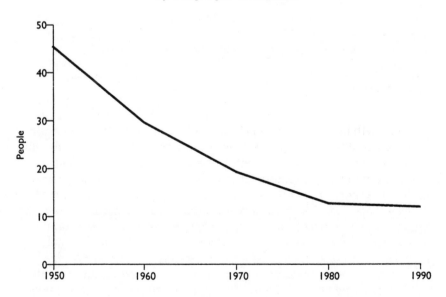

Source: 'Vital Signs' 1992, in UK Environmental Foresight Project

Figure 4.11 Numbers of automobiles worldwide, 1950–1990

of East Asia, are experiencing higher rates of pollution than this economic activity itself would seem to suggest. The amount of sulphur dioxide, nitrogen dioxide and suspended particulates, three of the most dangerous industrial pollutants, increased by a factor of ten in Thailand, eight in the Philippines and five in Indonesia, between 1975 and 1988. Five of the seven cities in the world with the worst air pollution are now in Asia (see Figure 4.12). In China the problem is probably of an even greater magnitude. The newspaper *China Daily* recently reported that almost sixty per cent of the country's urban water pollution could be traced to the three major cities. Urban areas facing grave air pollution included Shanghai, Jiangsu, Henan, Shandong, Beijing and Sichuan. The rural industries in these areas were also a source of serious air and water pollution. Rural industries produced 57.2 per cent of the pollutants piped into the air. Many of the small industries in these areas had out-of-date production technology and a high rate of waste discharge (*China Daily* 1993). The only effective way to deal with the problems generated by waste disposal and pollution on the scale suggested is to adopt advanced waste disposal techniques, and technologies which shift the emphasis from the treatment of discharges to cleaner production. This issue is returned to in the final chapter.

With energy demand in Asia doubling every 12 years, at current rates Asian countries will by 2005 produce more sulphur dioxide than Europe and North America combined. In addition, as we have noted, the number of motor vehicles in East Asia is doubling every seven years. Most of these vehicles use particularly dirty fuel, so bringing levels of pollution down to those of economic growth (perhaps 10 per cent per annum) would be a very significant achievement in itself.

There are immediate reasons for wanting to curb these levels of pollution in cities, apart from their contribution to global climate. In recent years, infant mortality levels have declined in East Asia, but ill health caused by pollution in Bangkok alone costs as much as $3 billion (US) each year, according to *The Economist* (1993). Currently the cost of pollution in large Asian cities is almost 10 per cent of gross domestic product. This is largely attributable to the use of old plant. The introduction of new, cleaner, industrial plant is much less than that for refitting old factories and redressing existing damage. This should provide an additional stimulus to manufacture, and transfer new, cleaner, technologies, rather than place the emphasis on short-term abatement policies.

Perhaps the most serious example of the way international political economy influences the disposal of wastes, is in the treatment of toxic

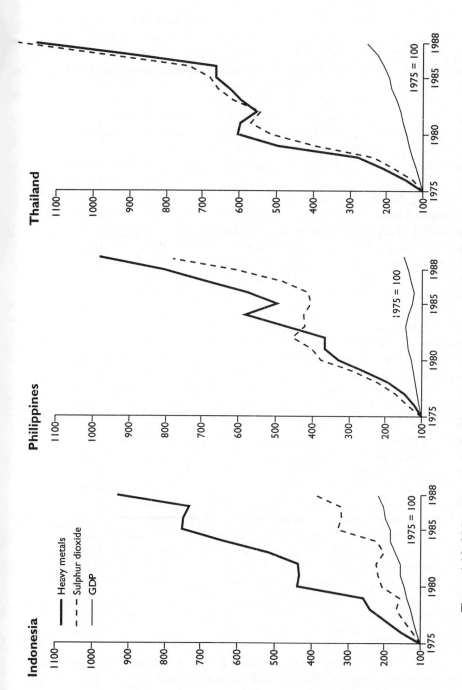

Figure 4.12 GDP and output of pollutants in Indonesia, the Philippines and Thailand, 1975–1988

substances. The export of toxic wastes from the North to the countries of the South is a response to economic factors. It is also a response, ironically, to the environmental concerns over toxic waste disposal in the industrialised countries. As the framework of regulation in the North has become tighter, waste management companies have actively sought sites for dumping toxic wastes, in order to lower their costs and improve their profitability. Most poor countries have relatively weak environmental regulations, and need the foreign exchange generated by waste traders.

Although developing countries need the income to be gained from accepting toxic waste from the North, they are rarely in a position to handle the effect of these wastes on peoples' health or the natural environment. Since 1989 the legal framework governing the inter-national trade in toxic wastes has been dictated, in theory, by the Basle Convention on the Transboundary Movement of Hazardous Waste and its Disposal. However, since 1989 the waste traders have sought to adopt new tactics to circumvent the regulatory framework of the Basle Convention. By early 1994, as a result of nearly a decade of campaigning, an alliance of Third World non-governmental organisations had successfully convinced the parties to the Basle Convention that they should ban all trade in waste with developing countries. However, waste traders have been astute in moving their operations to regions where environmental groups and the media are not active. Ultimately, the only way of ensuring that the trade in toxic wastes disappears, is to improve production processes in the North, and the management of waste there. Indeed, it can be argued that it is necessary to develop global co-operation in banning the waste trade, before cleaner production in the North can be placed on a proper footing (Clapp 1994).

In the meantime there is evidence that waste traders are exploiting a loophole in the Basle Convention, by describing waste exports to developing countries as substances intended for recycling or as foreign aid in the form of recoverable materials. It was recently reported in the British press that, in 1993, Britain exported 106,000 tonnes of waste, half of it to South East Asia, a figure three times higher than it had been just three years before. According to Customs records there were sixty-five developing countries receiving waste from the United Kingdom in 1993. The map below gives some indication of the locations which are used for dumping waste in the South (Figure 4.13).

This chapter has examined the relationship between the evolution of an industrial model based on hydrocarbons, which has fuelled

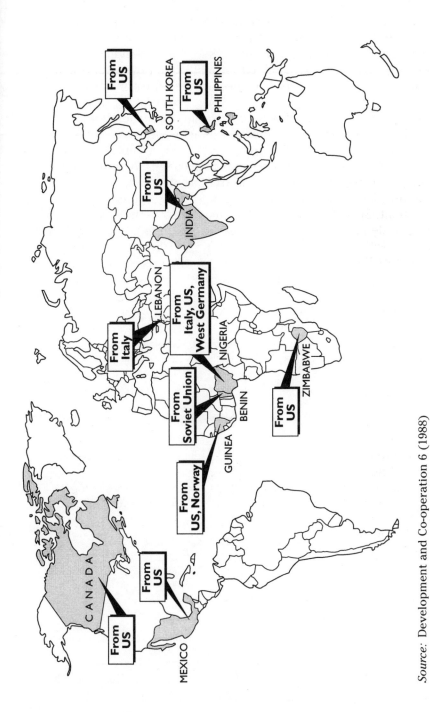

Source: Development and Co-operation 6 (1988)

Figure 4.13 Major international transfers of hazardous wastes

global consumption, and the environmental costs of this model. It has concentrated particularly on the way that the global political economy is developing, seeing increased consumption, and the production of wastes in the North, as indissolubly linked to the environmental problems of the South, sometimes directly... but always indirectly.

We have seen that it is not only the volume of consumption which is increasing – and with it the volume of wastes – but also the kinds of product and service which are consumed. In Chapters Six and Seven we explore the social processes which effectively turn political and economic relations into underlying social commitments, practices and cultures. But first we need to examine the way that the problems of consumption, and the role of global sinks such as the Amazon, are framed by national policies which pay little attention to the issue of global sustainability.

Chapter Five
Managing Global Resources

The environmentalist case is still largely 'reactive', and confined largely to the negative consequences of current policies: areas in which human behaviour jeopardises our resource base. The emphasis in the Green case is placed on our responsibilities to the environment and, in a broader sense, the species. However, it has been suggested that the role of consumption in the way we construct environmental problems, and the margins within which we deal with them, is still inadequately recognised. This chapter examines the policies which lie behind present levels of consumption.

In Chapter Three we examined the way that societies set their environmental 'targets' and the difficulty of establishing ground rules for sustainable development which can win broad public support and compliance. In this chapter we examine the way that the global environmental problem is framed. The cases considered focus upon energy policies, in the European Union and Brazil, as exemplifying the need not only to pursue 'sustainable' goals (as discussed in Chapter Three) but also the effect of considering these goals at different physical and geographical levels: the local, national and global. As we saw in Chapter Four, the pursuit of sustainable development cannot be divorced from international political economy. The 'problem' of global sustainability is framed by the existing relations of power which govern global economic interdependence. The way that obligations to the global environment are perceived depends on the way that these obligations are viewed from different regions, from a quite different economic perspective. We need to explore public policy – in Western Europe and Brazil – to understand the factors which are helping to construct the global agenda.

EUROPEAN ENERGY POLICY AND GLOBAL CHANGE

Concern with the possibility of global warming has refocused attention within the European Community on energy policy, and the best combination of policy instruments to reduce carbon emissions. To what extent can the tension between the need to protect the environment and the requirement for industrial innovation in the energy sector be resolved, and what are the benefits of a regulatory regime which has the support of the energy utilities? Policy in the European Union points to different answers depending on how the problem is framed. The future of European energy policy is only rarely considered from within a global perspective.

As we saw in Chapter Four, the rate of primary energy consumption to real gross domestic product (GDP) has been falling since about 1920 in most of the industrialised countries. Between 1973 and 1990 the energy used in these countries to produce a unit of output fell by one fifth (Figure 4.1). There are a number of reasons for this trend towards more energy efficient production. Technological innovation has reduced energy consumption in heavy industry. At the same time the shift away from heavy industry in the OECD countries, the rise in prices in the 1970s, and the expansion of the service sector, has accelerated this process.

As Frances Cairncross (1991) has previously argued, energy is still underpriced, creating a barrier to greater energy efficiency and better energy conservation. Before unification, West Germany spent $US 6 billion a year in subsidies to coal, forcing power companies to buy coal at prices well above market levels and reimbursing them through a levy of 8.5 per cent on consumers' electricity bills. Other European countries, such as Spain, France and Belgium, use similar devices. Since January 1993 the United Kingdom has followed suit. Although West European countries have not pursued energy-saving policies with the attention they might demand, their record is comparatively good if we consider East European countries. It is in Eastern Europe, under Soviet-style command economies, that cheap energy has been pursued at greater cost, particularly in environmental costs. This produced the severe environmental problems with which we have become more familiar since 1989, but has still not forced the

discontinuation of energy-wasteful technologies like the open-he _ ..
furnace, in many countries.

Energy, Efficiency and Global Warming: the 'Externality' Problem

The trend to greater energy efficiency in the developed OECD countries may be heading in the right direction: but is it enough to significantly reduce the risk of global warming? To what extent is better energy conservation a goal of European policy, and to what extent does this require new policy instruments?

Although controversy surrounds many of the calculations, it is clear that the Northern industrialised countries need to make dramatic progress in energy conservation if they are to stabilise atmospheric 'greenhouse' emissions. Perhaps even more importantly, their success in doing so is essential to any negotiated convention on global warming, like that of the Montreal Protocol (1987) to reduce CFC production. The developing countries of the South are often unwilling to make energy conservation a priority. Subsidies to commercial energy are often huge in developing countries. At the same time the energy technologies they come to depend upon, in the course of their development, are dirty and inefficient. Even to stabilise atmospheric greenhouse gas emission, that is to reduce the rate of their increase, means that today's output of 6 billion tons of carbon dioxide (or equivalent) needs to fall to about 1 billion tons.

The problem for the generation of energy in Europe is that most companies investing in energy expect a very much higher rate of return from their investments than from exploiting new forms of energy supply. Companies making energy-saving investments typically expect to recover their costs in two to three years, a 30 per cent internal rate of return. In contrast, the same companies may expect a much lower rate of return from new energy supplies, such as opening a new coal mine or building a new power station (Cairncross 1991). In this case the internal rate of return is often as low as five per cent. Clearly investment criteria are skewed in favour of costly energy generation. Many electricity companies in Europe, as well as state-owned utilities, believe there is no economic incentive to them to reduce their customers' energy consumption. Indeed, their effort continues to go into ways of expanding their consumption.

This makes it difficult to meet the obligations of a 'no regrets' strategy to reduce carbon emissions from the energy sector. As Angela Liberatore (1994) has argued, to become policy issues, climatological findings on global warming needed to be translated into 'manageable' interventions by the European Union. Previous community policies provided the 'frames' within which 'no regrets' policies could be pursued. Research on the economic policy and technological aspects of climate change promoted by the European Commission and national governments in Europe should help policy makers to design and select policy instruments for tackling the greenhouse effect. Energy policy has, as it were, been taken out of mothballs, to address the objectives of EU policy, particularly in the international sphere, where global warming is of paramount importance.

The Characteristics of the European Electricity Sector

Table 5.1 shows the production of electricity in Western Europe in 1990. Table 5.2 indicates the market for the electricity industries in Europe in the same year. These tables show that within the then European Community, conventional thermal power stations still provided the majority of electricity generated. (The only exceptions are France and Belgium, with their commitment to a vast programme of nuclear energy generation). The variations in per capita energy consumption in Table 5.2 reflect levels of economic development, and the size of the industrial sector, as well as the standard of living of European citizens.

What these tables do not reveal is that the energy sector in Europe has been subjected to two rather different influences. On the one hand, national governments have tended to develop close relations with their energy industries, irrespective of the balance of ownership between public and private. On the other hand, the European Community sought to pursue two policy goals that are not always convergent: the integration of the sector throughout the Community, and its deregulation. Most national governments have opposed Community intervention in energy policy. However, international pressures make this increasingly unrealistic. If we consider the consequence of energy consumption, in particular global warming, even the frame provided by the European Union is inadequate. We need to begin to pose the problem at the global level.

There are a number of common features to the European energy sector, as noted by McGowan (1992):

1. There has been considerable consolidation, as small electricity companies have been absorbed by larger ones.

Table 5.1 Energy production in Europe, 1990

	Production (GWh)			
Country	Hydraulic	Conventional	Nuclear	Total
Germany	17,645	259,633	139,237	416,515
Belgium	894	25,719	40,547	67,160
Denmark	528	23,265	–	23,893
Spain	25,810	65,494	51,959	143,263
France	57,010	45,190	297,825	400,025
Greece	1,981	30,060	–	32,041
Holland	168	65,703	3,296	69,167
Ireland	984	12,723	–	13,707
Italy	34,809	171,633	–19	206,423
Luxembourg	803	518	–	1,321
Portugal	9,140	17,624	–	26,764
UK	6,940	232,347	58,779	298,066
EEC	156,712	950,009	591,624	1,698,345

Source: McGowen 1992

Table 5.2 Energy demand in Europe, 1990

Country	Energy demand (GWh)	Extension (km²)	Population (millions)	Consumption per capita* (kWh/person/year)
Germany	411,252	356,828	77.8	5,286
Belgium	62,618	30,518	9.9	6,295
Denmark	30,987	43,076	5.1	6,034
Spain	141,485	504,782	38.9	3,635
France	349,091	543,965	56.3	6,200
Greece	32,452	131,990	10.0	3,230
Holland	78,374	41,160	14.9	5,263
Ireland	13,300	70,283	3.5	3,793
Italy	236,350	301,263	57.6	4,105
Luxembourg	4,184	2,586	0.4	11,057
Portugal	26,597	91,987	10.3	2,573
UK	307,430	244,023	57.4	5,355
EEC	1,694,120	2,362,461	342.1	4,949

Source: UNESA data – measured by the energy available for the market in power station bars, cited in McGowen 1992

2. There has been continuing public participation, often accompanying programmes of privatisation.
3. There is more centralisation and integration within the energy sector than is revealed by ownership structures alone.
4. Despite lowered investment recently, the energy utilities still command enormous investment programmes: over £4 billion annually in the United Kingdom, France, Germany and Italy.

On the whole, the interests of the energy sector and those of national governments have been seen as synonymous in Europe. Indeed, governments have sought to use the electricity industry as an adjunct of economic policy, such as policy on inflation. The question that remains is whether national governments will prove as willing to use their close links with the energy sector to pursue environmental policies, such as measures to slow global warming. Their willingness to act in this way may in part depend on the extent to which the Single European Market, and other integrative policies, enable energy overcapacity in one country to be matched, in a co-ordinated way, with undercapacity in others.

European Protection and the Energy Sector in the European Community

The Fourth European Community Environmental Action Programme (1987–1992) contained four principles: preventive action; the 'polluter pays'; rectifying pollution at source; and the principle of integrating environmental policy into other European Community policies. This fourth principle is obviously of particular importance in relation to the energy sector. It was given added force by two articles of the Single European Act (100A and 13OR-T) which provide the legal basis for a community policy on environmental interventions.

The Community recognised, if somewhat belatedly, that many of the dynamic effects of greater economic integration, including those of the energy sector, are likely to carry damaging environmental consequences. At the same time, fiscal harmonisation policies within the Community have enormous environmental implications. Harmonisation needs to take account of whether goods and services are environmentally friendly or damaging (Delbeke 1991). The consequences of economic growth are likely to include increased carbon emissions unless fiscal measures can be used to increase energy conservation dramatically. Only economic recession in the early 1990s obscured the global environmental effects of the stimulus provided by greater economic integration in Europe. Without economic recession the European Union would not have met its modest undertaking, under the Framework Climate Convention, to meet 1990 levels of emission by the year 2000.

At the same time, other aspects of energy generation have met more resistance from environmentalists, and the public at large. Operational limitations have emerged in the construction of larger power stations and their location. Nuclear generation, attractive in terms of reducing global warming, is associated with other environmental problems. Europe's energy utilities are thus increasingly affected by shifts in public perceptions. Environmental objectives to the supply-side technology are matched by Community-level policies to reduce the over-supply of energy and increase efficiency in its production. The fall in energy prices from the mid-1980s marked the end of the 'scarcity culture' of the 1970s. The 'limits to growth' in the 1990s appear to have less to do with limits in the resources available for growth than with the environmental consequences of growth (Meadows, Meadows and Randers 1992). The consequences of these shifts, in public perception and European policy, for the energy sector are vitally important. If energy is not a 'special case', but like any other commodity, can it be regulated at will? If it is a special case what can we do to ensure that the production of valued commodities does not imperil the wider sustainability of the planet?

Regulation and Abatement Expenditures in the European Energy Sector

Expenditure on pollution abatement still represents a very small percentage of gross domestic product in most European countries. Even in the Netherlands, where the National Environment Plan is one of the most comprehensive ever published, abatement expenditure is still expected to be only 4 per cent of GDP in 2010. In most OECD countries, abatement expenditure today is less than 2 per cent of GDP.

The effect of abatement measures on economic growth is probably modest, and certainly much less than the effects on growth of environmental damage. Indeed environmental abatement measures are, in many ways, a necessary stimulus to sustainable growth. Rothwell (1992) reports the results of regulation in an interesting paper. His evidence suggests that the existence of regulations does not necessarily mean that market-orientated innovation was held back. Rather, it was the nature of the regulations, the behaviour of regulatory agencies and the relationship between regulators and regulated, that caused most problems.

The role of economic incentives and disincentives in encouraging more efficient energy production, and consumption, has attracted considerable interest recently. Direct regulation involves governments imposing a legally enforceable standard which must be met. The use of economic incentives, including fiscal interventions such as carbon or energy taxes, is according to neo-classical theory, essentially an attempt to promote allocative efficiency. It is widely argued that this approach encourages the more efficient allocation of resources and offers greater opportunities for innovation. If you tax a product you change its price, and affect trade flows. Harmonisation is therefore a condition of an internal market like that of the EU, where products are intended to be freely tradeable. The logic of economic liberalisation across energy markets, therefore, is to place increasing pressure on individual countries to 'internalise' environmental costs while remaining competitive.

However, if you tax or charge an emission you are affecting a factor of production, a natural resource. As Europe moves towards a mix of policy instruments for combating environmental externalities, carbon budgets for individual countries, and for the Union as a whole, can play a larger part in setting the terms of the energy policy debate. These would 'allocate' permissible levels of carbon emissions to individual countries, linked to their population size. Increasingly technical innovation in energy generation, as well as economies on the demand side, will be seen as a vehicle of wider European policy. Broadly speaking, the critical period in which fossil fuels are phased out is between now and the middle of the next century.

We need to demonstrate progress in developing and transferring cleaner energy technologies to the developing world, without impeding their economic development, if we are to make any significant steps towards halting global warming. It will take time to decommission traditional power stations in the North: time which should be spent developing alternatives for utilisation in the South. At the diplomatic level, international agreement on climate change depends upon European countries demonstrating their seriousness in achieving the targets agreed at the Earth Summit in Rio de Janeiro in 1992. Although the role of the energy utilities in this process is merely part of the solution, it is, arguably, the most important part (Table 5.3). European governments can no longer afford to be the 'defenders' of national energy policies that pay scant attention to the European, and still more, global, dimensions. The requirements of

Table 5.3 Carbon dioxide emissions, 1990 (United Kingdom)

	By source		By final energy consumer	
	MtC	%	MtC	%
Power stations	54	34	–	–
Refineries	5	3	–	–
Households	22	14	41	26
Industry & agriculture	37	23	56	35
Commercial & public sector	8	5	24	15
Road transport	30	19	33	21
Other transport	4	2	5	3
Total:	160		159	

CO_2 emission estimates are derived from energy consumption data. UK CO_2 emissions in 1990 totalled 160 million tonnes of carbon MtC. This table shows UK CO_2 emissions in 1990 by source (that is according to where the fuel is first used). For households, industry and agriculture, and the commercial and public sectors, this excludes emissions attributable to their use of electricity. It also shows emissions in 1990 with power station, refinery and other fuel-processing emissions attributed to the end users of the energy.

Source: Climate Change, UK National Programme for CO_2 Emissions. Department of Environment 1993.

technological innovation in the energy sector, and the research which underpins technology and environmental policy, increasingly point to a much-needed convergence of European energy policy and the establishment of environmental objectives for the European Union as a whole.

The example of European energy policy, and its environmental context, illustrates the limitations of conceiving of sustainable development as an 'addition' or 'modification' to current policy. Unless the problem of global sustainability is put squarely into the frame, policy at the level of the European Union will be designed to encourage convergence of national and Union-wide practices. The contribution of these policies to the larger, global, canvas will be ignored.

SUSTAINABLE ENERGY POLICIES FOR THE BRAZILIAN AMAZON

There are many misconceptions about the Amazon, some of them held by governments in the region. The popular view is that most of the Amazon rainforest is being cut down, that pressure from international banks has led to the conversion of land for hydropower, that local populations, left to their own devices, would act more 'sustainably'. Each of these statements is, at best, a half-truth. None of them do justice to the complexity of the issues.

Looked at from space, the Amazon corresponds to one twentieth of the Earth's land surface, two-fifths of South America's surface area, and three-fifths of Brazil. The Amazon also contains one-fifth of the globe's fresh water resources, and half of the tropical forest. The population of the Brazilian Amazon, currently 17 million, is increasing at over one million a year. Because of the scale and global importance of the Amazon region, the decisions made by one country, Brazil, carry implications for the rest of humanity. This places particular responsibility on ensuring that a sustainable energy policy can be developed for the region.

Constraints on a Sustainable Energy Policy for the Amazon

There are a number of important constraints on the development of sustainable energy policies for the Amazon. These include:

- **Population growth** In 1990 Brazil's population was growing at 1.7 per cent a year. In the 1980s it grew at 1.9 per cent a year. In 2015 Brazil's population will be growing at about 1.3 per cent a year. In 1992 the population stood at 152 million. In 2020 it is expected to be 234 million. More people means a greatly increased demand for energy; higher living standards for the Brazilian majority mean much more energy will be consumed.
- **Economic growth** Following its current economic model, if Brazil is to meet the energy demands of its economy it will need to develop the Amazon Basin. The Brazilian economy will grow by about 3.5 per cent in 1993. As Table 5.4 shows, population increase alone implies that installed energy capacity will need to increase by nearly 50 per cent in the next thirty years. In addition, an increase in energy consumption per capita during this period will require a much greater installed capacity; almost four times that of 1990. If economic growth continues at about 4 per cent, it is quite possible for Brazil to meet increased demand for energy. However, energy consumption levels like that of France will require major exploitation of hydropower in the Amazon region. By 2020 the Amazon could account for over half the installed capacity of the country (see Table 5.4).

Table 5.4 Brazilian energy consumption, 1990–2020

	1990	2020	2020[1]
Population	150 million	234 million	234 million
Energy consumption (GW)	1.1	1.1	3.0
Installed capacity (GW)	50	71	194
Amazonian contribution (GW)	4.3	15	100

1 If energy consumption in Brazil equalled that of France
* Tons of petroleum equivalent per person, per annum

Source: Di Lascio and Di Lascio (1993)

- **International opinion**   Because of the size of the Amazon, and its importance for carbon sequestration, and as a reservoir of biodiversity, international public opinion frequently claims some degree of tacit sovereignty over the Amazon. It is suggested that the Amazon is a global resource, a common property resource on the global scale. This view is contested in Brazil, where the 'occupation' of the Amazon by Brazilians is looked upon as a necessary prerequisite for any national planning of the region. The depredations of foreign companies, and the clamour of environmentalists, is seen by many in Brazil as proof that the Amazon cannot be entrusted to the international community.

One of the difficulties encountered in preparing a sustainable energy policy for the Amazon, as a recent report to the President demonstrated, is that a sustainable energy policy for the Amazon can mean at least one of three things (Pedasa 1993):

1. It can refer to the sustainable development of energy resources in the Amazon region.
2. It can refer to the contribution of the Amazon region to sustainable development in Brazil.
3. It can also refer to the contribution of the Amazon to the sustainable development of the globe.

These dimensions are frequently confused, both within Brazil, and outside it. They also illustrate the way in which the problem of energy needs and environmental destruction are framed in different ways, by different groups of people. The 'problem' of sustainable develop-

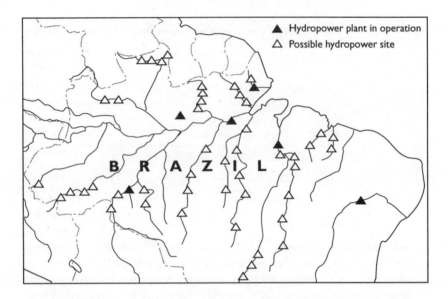

Figure 5.1 The location of hydropower plants in the Amazon

ment of the Amazon region is perceived as quite different from the role of the Amazon in the sustainable development of Brazil.

Energy Policy Options for Brazil

Over 95 per cent of Brazil's commercial energy is generated from hydropower. Before considering the future development of this resource, it is worth considering the alternative sources of energy available to Brazil.

Coal   Brazil possesses only limited coal reserves, and these are located in the south of the country, in Rio Grande Do Sul. In 2015 Brazil expects to be importing energy, including coal from Colombian mines.

Other Hydrocarbons   The mining of hydrocarbons is of growing importance in the Amazon region as a whole. Colombia, Ecuador and Peru discovered important Amazon deposits in the 1960s, although smaller deposits had been discovered previously. In Bolivia, oil and gas production began in the Department of Santa Cruz. In Peru, Petroleos Del Peru has demonstrated proven reserves of 340 million barrels, with unproven reserves of almost 2 billion barrels. In 1987

Brazil discovered oil and gas deposits in the Urucu River, a tributary of the Jurua River, and exploitation has been carried out in Acre, between Manaus and Santarem, and in the mouth of the Amazon. The estimated reserves in the state of Acre are six billion tons, but annual production is still small. Petrobras has made significant offshore oil discoveries over the past twenty years. However, the evidence suggests that proven reserves in Brazil have a lifespan of only six years or so, at present rates of consumption, if no oil were imported.

The present natural gas reserves from Jurua and Urucu total 41 billion cubic metres. Petrobras estimates that natural gas production could reach about 3.5 million cubic metres per day by 1995, and about 8.2 million cubic metres per day by 2000. Petrobras and Electronorte, still part of the state-owned electricity utility, have made joint studies of the potential for using natural gas in combined-cycle gas-turbine plant in Manaus and Porto Velho. The natural gas could be transported by gas pipeline, or by barge in liquified form.

Nuclear   Brazil has a large nuclear programme, but it is widely perceived as enormously wasteful and carries unacceptable risks, especially within the context of fragile ecological systems like that of the Amazon. There might, however, be a small role for nuclear energy in Brazil, in the longer term.

Biomass   The contribution of biomass to Brazil's energy matrix is declining. The investment in different sources of energy between 1978 and 1987 was much greater in hydro (59 per cent of the total) than in petroleum (28 per cent) or biomass (8 per cent). Nevertheless between 1975 and 1992, over $US 18 billion was invested in the ethanol programmes in Brazil, of which infrastructure alone accounted for almost half. The ethanol programme is one of the most dramatic, if not necessarily most successful, attempts to develop energy from biomass, in this case sugar cane.

The potential of biomass energy sources for a country with a vast land mass, like Brazil's, cannot be ignored. In Amazonia, extensive areas are covered with native palm trees, notably buriti (*Mauritia* spp) on an estimated 8 million hectares, and babacu (*Orbignya* spp) with 14 million hectares. These could yield, annually, 40 million and 5 million metric tons of vegetable oil, respectively (Molion 1993). These oils could be used as fuel in diesel engines for generating electricity and transportation, promoting regional development.

There have also been several small-scale experiments using natural forest timber to generate electrical energy, and another medium-scale experiment using wood byproducts as an electrical power source. Electronorte operated two 7.5 megawatt woodburning thermal plants during the construction of Balbina and Samuel dams to supply electricity to the construction sites. The results from the three projects demonstrated that cutting, transporting and burning natural tropical woods, to generate electrical energy, cost about twice that of electricity generated from diesel fuel (Cadman 1993). Manufacturers of diesel engines could adapt vehicles for vegetable oil sources, as car manufacturers have adapted engines for ethanol.

The case for more use of bioenergy is a strong one. As a recent United Nations report puts it:

> One of the most important points (of principle) is that bioenergy is essentially a low-cost decentralized technology ... Biofuel systems can often be installed quickly and cheaply; and they can be installed in regions where the energy they produce is needed.
>
> (UNEP 1991).

For these reasons the contribution of biomass to the energy needs of the Amazon region, if not Brazil as a whole, cannot be ignored.

The Development of Hydropower in Brazil

Hydroelectric power is likely to remain, in the long term, Brazil's principal source of energy. As Cadman has demonstrated, growing energy demands in Brazil will place ever greater demands on the Amazon region. However, it is important to recognise that these energy demands are linked to a specific economic model; they are not immutable.

Brazil currently has an installed capacity of 50 GW (gigawatts), most of which is provided by dams in the south, southeast or northern states. The current intention is to double installed capacity by the year 2000, when hydro is still expected to account for over 90 per cent of installed capacity. At the present time nearly three-quarters of Brazil's energy comes from only ninety plants. Moreover, Brazil's hydro plants are low-cost, and they are increasingly being developed for multiple uses of the available water resources.

The energy-generating potential of southeast Brazil has almost been exhausted. Increasingly, power will be piped into heavily populated areas from the south and the Amazon, where the potential is high. It has been estimated by Electrobras that over half the remaining hydro potential in Brazil is in the Amazon, much of it in the state of Para. As the head of Electrobras has put it, 'the utilization of Amazonian hydropower is driven by the whole nation, not the local communities of the region' (Filho 1993).

As we have seen, nuclear energy is subject to increased public scrutiny, and hydrocarbon supplies are not nearly large enough to cope with growing demand. An estimated 80 per cent of the funds for meeting future energy demand in Brazil will have to come from tariffs, leaving only 20 per cent to the international development bank. Because of its unusually high reliance on hydro, Brazil's contribution to greenhouse gas emissions is relatively low. Brazil releases only 7 kilograms of carbon per megawatt of power generated, compared with an average 170 kg per MW for developing countries as a whole (whose dependence on biomass is much greater, at about 35 per cent of energy generated (Moreira 1993).

Hydropower in the Amazon Basin

The first hydroelectrical power plants to be built in the Amazon came into service in 1975 (Cadman 1989). They were the 40 MW Curua-Una plant, near the city of Santarem, in the state of Para, and the 40 MW Coaracy Nunes plant on the Araguari River, which supplies power to the city of Macapa in the state of Amapa. This second plant is owned by Electronorte, one of the regional power companies still under state ownership.

In 1976, construction began of the Tucurui Dam, part of the Amazon Basin's first large hydroelectric development. At the peak of construction in 1981 there were almost 22,000 workers employed on this project. The population of the residential town constructed near the site of the dam for the workers and their families rose to over 50,000. The Tucurui Dam is located on the Tocantins River, 300 kilometres south of Belem, the capital city of Para (see Figure 5.1). As in much of the Amazon, the remoteness of the site produced substantial logistical difficulties. Access to the site was only possible by a dirt road 500 kilometres long, or a 400-kilometre river barge trip. The plant supplies electrical energy to the cities of Belem and Sao Luis, the vast Carajas iron mine, two aluminium smelters and the north-eastern grid. In other words Tucurui was established to meet Brazil's industrial production targets. Its main objective was to supply energy for the mining and metallurgic companies in Amazonia. The Tucurui project prompted widespread social resistance in Amazonia, on the part of social groups who felt their sustainable activities were taking second place to the extravagant industrial model of Amazonian development.

Three years later the 250 MW Balbina Dam, located on the Uatuma River, in the middle of the tropical rainforest, came into operation. The Balbina complex supplies energy to the fast-growing city of Manaus, capital city of the state of Amazonas, which lies 150 kilometres to the south-east (see Figure 5.1). A 70 kilometre access road to the site had to be built especially for this project. The construction of the Balbina complex necessitated the flooding of a vast area of tropical forest, 2360 square kilometres in extent. Like other dams at Samuel and San Antonio, considerable opposition began to be mounted to the project, reflecting the very considerable environmental effects of each project, and the social resistance from the 'development' process. For them, the grandiose industrial designs of Brazil's leaders, rather than the sustainable development of the Amazon itself, was the key issue.

Environmental Conflicts in the Amazon

Fears about the effects of large dams in the Amazon have been fuelled by evidence from satellite images. Calculations from remote sensing suggest that about 120,000 square kilometres of forest was burned in 1988 alone. Forest destruction during the last two decades indicates that about one-tenth of the Amazon forest may have been destroyed. Satellite images show millions of square kilometres of fire-clouds over the western Amazon every July and August, the season for forest burning. During one day in August 1993, 83,000 fires were recorded from space, in the Brazilian Amazon. On another day, 101,000 fires were identified. These data are communicated to the Brazilian Space Institute, and to the relevant government departments within twenty minutes of being registered by satellite.

To understand the real significance of this kind of data, however, we need to understand the causes of forest burning in Amazonia (Molion 1993). Some of the fires are in savannah areas, where forest fires occur naturally. Even in forested areas we need to distinguish between fires resulting from burning brushwood and undergrowth, and those resulting from new tree-felling. Only an estimated 10,000 square kilometres a year can be attributed to new deforestation in the Brazilian Amazon. Of the area which has already been deforested, almost one-third is burned annually. In July and August, when the forest is at its driest, this figure will be at its highest. At other times, deforested areas burn two or three times a year, often through accidents or vandalism. Today, forest fires signalling the destruction of new areas reach into other Amazonian countries. One of the most important of these is Paraguay, where no systematic monitoring of forest fires is undertaken.

Although forest fires in the Brazilian Amazon represent a very large proportion of the global total, we should not lose sight of the fact that they contribute relatively little to global emissions of carbon dioxide. In 1988, forest burning in Brazil generated about 1 per cent of world emissions, as Cadman points out, considerably less than the 25 per cent generated by the United States (Cadman, 1989). However, the destruction of tropical forest areas involves other fears, which are more difficult to allay, including the polluting effects of mercury-sluicing activities for gold, open-cast mining operations, the forced resettlement of people and the demise of indigenous cultures (Zylberstajn and Souza 1993). Although it is unrealistic to try to preserve the Amazon Basin in its original, untouched state, Brazil's growing population and increased demand for energy will, perforce, carry implications for the future development of the Amazon. Even if the rest of Brazil had no additional energy needs, demand in the Amazon area alone would require a considerable increase in power generation.

There is now a very considerable literature concerning the environmental impacts of resource use in the Amazon. Most writers, like Smith, point out that the environmental effect of development schemes and spontaneous settlement have regional and global implications (Smith et al 1991). The realities accompanying the designation of 'reserved area' status, for humans as well as ecological systems, involve political complexities and continuous monitoring (IDB 1991). As Richard Norgaard observed, well over a decade ago, the sustainable development of the Amazon requires what he termed 'co-evolution' between the ecological system of the region, and the cultural and economic systems which are acquiring dominance (Norgaard 1981). Physical geographers like Eden (1990) have demonstrated why the necessary co-evolution will be difficult to achieve, given the principles that underlie Amazonian ecology (Eden 1988).

Sustainable energy policies for the Brazilian Amazon, based on the provision of alternative sources of energy, including biomass and small-scale hydropower, are not an impossible dream, but they do require a large measure of policy integration and political will (Mougeot 1985). They also require more than the compliance of the people affected: without the full participation of interested groups in the planning of their own communities, internal opposition and external criticism will probably make energy policy unworkable in Brazil. In this sense the Amazon is a model not only for how tropical forest regions should develop sustainably, but also for wider, global, attempts at sustainable development.

The Amazon basin is clearly a critical zone at the global level. It contains a high proportion of species diversity in its tropical ecosystems; it is a significant 'sink' for the sequestration of carbon. However, the issues that come into play when the development of the Amazon is discussed are rarely global. Brazil receives little benefit from finding a global resource, and global sink, within its territory. The sovereignty of Brazilian institutions, however, is also at stake. Critics of the Brazilian state argue, convincingly, that the kind of development represented by the Tucurui dam is unsustainable. However, the Tucurui dam is linked to Brazil's insertion within a wider economic nexus. Energy consumption in Brazil, including that of poor people marginalised from many of the 'benefits' of development, is linked to an economic model that places economic profitability at the level of the world system above the conservation of a global resource. A global sink is being destroyed in the interests of Brazil's global integration within markets for minerals and bauxite.

The 'problem' does not originate in Brazil; it is structured around the unsustainable pathways of global interdependence, as we saw in Chapter Four. In this chapter we have explored some of the ways in which national and even international policies are framed, without serious consideration being given to their pervasive, global, effects. In the next two chapters we examine the nature of global environmental management and the social preferences that enable individuals to distance themselves from the consequences of their actions.

Chapter Six
Metabolising Nature

The suggestion that we bear collective responsibility for environmental problems has almost become an axiom of modern life. However, it is a proposition that is rarely examined closely, free from rhetoric and moral opprobrium. In Chapters Three and Four we explored global economic relations and their environmental impact. The idea has gained currency that the solution to environmental problems lies at the global scale, where more and more 'problems' seem to lie. Global problems, runs the argument, require global solutions, which must begin with a distinct moral purpose and political resolution.

As we have seen, this was the message which was taken to the UNCED conference, although perhaps not the message that people brought away from it. Accord was sought on a series of international agreements which could put the stamp of sustainability on the political relations between states. In the event, of course, such ambitious hopes were dashed, and many of the more unrealistic expectations from Rio were quietly dropped. There have been various post-mortems on UNCED, and it is not being suggested that another is needed (O'Keefe et al 1993). What is needed, however, is a rigorous examination of the underlying forces at work, which serve to generate environmental problems at the global level, and the solutions which are currently offered to these problems. We need to ask whether global environmental management can be seen as the means of effecting changes, while the distribution of global resources is so unequal (Chapter Four).

This takes us, in this chapter, into the domain of consumption and the difficult political choices from which 'management' is supposed to release us. In the next chapter we consider the social commitments which drive consumption. It also leads us to question the pre-occupations of environmentalism itself, which seem to have left no clear trajectory, and even less political commitment, at the global level. Realism, at the international level, seems to mean global environmental management. But is such management possible? Is it workable? Perhaps we need to make fundamental shifts in the process of development before we can 'manage' the contradictions of the environment.

GLOBAL ENVIRONMENTAL MANAGEMENT

One of the best reports ever written on global environmental change, which was presented to the Netherlands government, is *Energy Policy in the Greenhouse* (1990). This report put the issue very succinctly:

> Much of the current climate warming debate still proceeds along the narrow lines of conventional air pollution abatement policy. But climate stabilization is an entirely different challenge. The greenhouse effect is driven by a confluence of environmental impacts that have their source not only in the nature of human resource use, but also in the current international economic order. Climate stabilization, therefore, requires a *comprehensive turn around towards environmentally sound and socially equitable development* – in short, an unprecedented North-South Compact on sustainable development. (Krause, Bach and Kooney 1990, 1.7–1).

The point to note about this quotation is that sustainable development is seen as the necessary *prerequisite* for global environmental agreements, rather than a longer-term goal, which might be pursued regardless of whether agreements are reached on the global agenda. Nothing that happened at UNCED alters the importance of this statement. The global agreements that were concluded have given rise to a series of reporting activities, and modest environmental targets, which most individual governments are showing little commitment to achieve. Moreover, such measures, including the agreement to limit carbon emissions to more manageable standards, do not address the underlying issue. This is the relationship between the pursuit of economic growth, and the implications of this growth for the way we 'metabolise' nature. We need to return to our model of industrial metabolism outlined in Chapter Three.

THE 'EMPTY' AND 'FULL' WORLD SYSTEM: A POINT OF DEPARTURE

Robert Goodland and colleagues (1992) have produced a useful diagram of the global ecosystem, which locates the growing economic subsystem within the larger picture (Figure 6.1). Their diagram shows the global ecosystem as a closed system: the only extraneous element being solar energy. Economies, and societies, grow by utilising the resources available to them, transforming these resources into commodities and services, and getting rid of the waste products. Waste is despatched into the sinks which are themselves part of the global ecosystem: oceans and rivers, land-fill and, particularly during the last century or so, the atmosphere.

We can begin by considering the way we read the Goodland/Daly diagram. On the whole our preoccupation with growth, and the satisfaction of material needs, has emphasised the source functions of the environment over its sink functions. This preoccupation has left us, theoretically, within the social sciences, without a theory of sinks. It is clear that the discussions at UNCED, and subsequently, have served to emphasise the importance to policy of global sinks. Most of the agreements that were signed, or proposed, for climate, biodiversity (and forests) sought to address the sink functions, that are performed by 'nature'. However, our theoretical understanding of the processes through which we manage and transform the environment, at the global scale, is limited to the pillage of what was taken (which we term 'imperialism') rather than what was left behind. We have no theory of sinks. These sinks are both 'global' to all of us and 'local' to some of us. The intellectual challenge lies in making the connection, and demonstrating its social consequences.

We can begin with the kind of economic (and social) systems which Daly and Goodland locate at the centre of human activities. Industrial systems are unlike those of nature, in that they are not closed, as we saw in Chapter Three. Within natural systems, biological processes

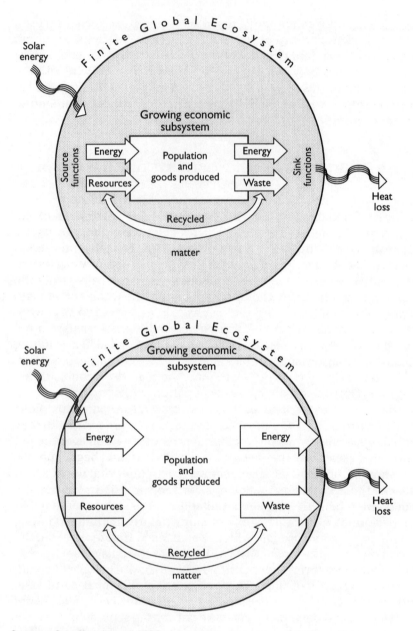

Source: Goodland et al 1992

Figure 6.1 The finite global ecosystem relative to the growing economic subsystem

serve to maintain the equilibrium of the total system, largely through recycling, as Robert Ayres has observed (Ayres 1994). Industrial systems, including the industrialised modern food system, do not recycle most of their wastes (Goodman and Redclift 1991). Instead 'nutrients' are converted into matter, and energy, which cannot be absorbed by the system itself. This observation lies behind a number of Green approaches, of course, principally Lovelock's notion of Gaia, which sees nature as exhibiting a self-regulating 'logic', which the human species is always in danger of ignoring (Lovelock 1995).

The growth of the economic sub-system implies two kinds of burden for the global ecosystem. First, of course, many resources are not renewable, and those that are renewable are frequently over-exploited. Second, as we have already observed, the resource base doubles as the sink in which we deposit our waste, our detritus. In as much as our economic activities are investigated for their sustainability, it is usually as resource systems that they are found wanting. The equally important sink functions are usually confined, and then only recently, to the global sphere. On the whole the canopy of environmental regulation that we have constructed to deal with our wastes, imposes penalties in one area that lead wastes to be redirected towards another: from air, to water, to land-fill (Ayres 1992). They rarely address the issue that lies behind these forms of regulation: the generation of waste implies a capacity on the part of the environment to assume uncosted sink functions.

It is clear that our patterns of consumption have not fully incorporated the value of these sink functions. In fact, we have barely started to internalise our externalities. In seeking to reach agreements about climate, and biodiversity, we are at least beginning to acknowledge that externalities can have implications that were barely considered a couple of decades ago. (Indeed, the 'limits to growth' debate was about the assumed limitations of resources, and made little reference to the capacities of sinks). These implications also have a momentum of their own, since they frequently involve disruptions in systems, which we do not fully understand, and cannot easily respond to.

It is suggested that unless we grasp the full implications of the total processes in the Goodland/Daly model, we will be unable to reach meaningful agreements at any level, including the international level. These processes bring two kinds of system into conflict: one that reproduces itself metabolically, and one that can only metabolise nature by leaving additional problems for us to address. Our ability to grasp the centrality of this contrast is also important for social theory, since a failure to recognise the realist agenda, on the part of the social sciences, is closely connected with the way they have evolved epistemologically. This debate between constructivism and critical realism is referred to in Chapter Seven.

Over a decade ago, Humphrey and Buttel expressed something of this concern when they wrote that sociology had indulged in a 'collective celebration of Western social institutions' in which 'assumptions that energy-intensive industrial development is the natural end point of a universal process of social evolution and modernization' have remained unchallenged (Humphrey and Buttel 1982). This observation is more accurate for sociology, perhaps, than some of the other social sciences, notably anthropology. But the force of the statement remains: until the Green perspective on development gains legitimacy (itself, perhaps a contradiction) our ideas, as well as our practices, will tend to reinforce the dominant model of growth, and perpetuate environmental problems at the global level. At the same time, the links between our material practices and the dependent ideology of consumerism, need much more attention than they have been given. We need to explore the relationship between the kinds of objectives set out in Rio: more effective measurement and valuation of the environment; greater democratic control; and the possibility of finding a balance between improvement in the standard of living and improvement in the quality of life.

HOW WE MEASURE ENVIRONMENTAL QUALITY: THE COSTS OF CONSUMPTION

During the last decade much more attention has been given to ways of assessing environmental quality, and the measures that need to be taken to preserve it. Work by natural scientists on 'critical loads' has assessed the point at which increasing levels of pollution can endanger ecosystems, usually within fairly wide bounds of uncertainty (Wynne 1994). The point at issue is that we are poorly placed to anticipate environmental changes, if we confine our assessment of dangers to single variables. This concern with the resilience of ecosystems has strengthened the need for the precautionary principle to be recognised, and to be incorporated in planning procedures (Jordan 1993).

The measurement of environmental degradation and losses has also led to the development of natural-resource accounting techniques, and the establishment of resource inventories, not simply for natural species, but in terms of the economic value of species and ecosystems. Environmental economics has provided a number of key procedures for assessing the losses to future generations from current decisions, the environmental value that is forgone by 'rational' economic behaviour in the marketplace, and the value which the public attaches to environmental goods and services (see Chapter Seven).

There are clearly ways in which such information can be useful. For industry, the acknowledgment of unseen environmental costs can represent a challenge to research and development. This is what the German sociologist Huber has termed 'ecological modernisation': the opportunity that modern production techniques afford to incorporate environmental considerations within the design and development of products. Advanced capitalism, according to this perspective, provides few problems that cannot be managed by better environmental management, perhaps through arriving at 'utilisation values', examining the life-cycle through which products and services pass. (Huber 1982).

Life-cycle analysis was originally developed by private industry, to reduce the costs of transporting domestic detergents, and can be seen as a commercial response to a new market opportunity. Aware that a sizeable part of the public, especially in Northern Europe, is interested in reducing domestic waste, recycling products, and using less energy, many large companies attach more importance to the 'environmental friendliness' of their products. In some segments of the market, quality commodities and services are increasingly associated with explicit environmental objectives. Companies that engage in environmental auditing, moreover, stand to save money as well as gaining in environmental credibility. If the system of market incentives and regulation can be changed to reflect this new corporate awareness, it is argued, we can envisage maintaining levels of consumption in more sustainable ways. Indeed, sustainable development has come to mean 'sustainable levels of consumption' in some quarters (Redclift 1993b). At an aggregated, national, level as we saw in Chapter Three, it is possible to develop 'sustainability indicators' which more fully reflect environmental costs and benefits in the calculation of national income.

A number of key questions remain, however. Natural-resource accounting, environmental auditing, the assessment of critical loads, life-cycle analysis and other similar techniques are just that, *techniques*. They are not measures to help us reach societal objectives, but management tools, which might assist in achieving such objectives once they have been defined. In the absence of clearly defined environmental objectives, and a clear vision of sustainable development, governments have tended to substitute their faith in environmental management for wider processes of political and social consultation. As Friends of the Earth observed, in their response to the British government's draft submission to the Commission for Sustainable Development, techniques are not a substitute for the clear definition of sustainability objectives.

At the same time, policy interventions to address environmental problems which fail to address causes, are likely to lead to what has been described as 'sub-optimal choices' (Ayres 1992, 16). Examples exist of policies which have redirected environmental burdens from one area to another, or instituted practices, such as 'clean coal' technology, which soon become institutionalised, and do nothing to prevent new forms of pollution. In some cases pollution is diverted geographically: from Western to Eastern Europe, or from developed to developing countries.

Many of the products, and services, which characterise ecological modernisation (and, of course, its counterpart 'green consumerism') represent institutionalised practices, and technologies, which merely shift the parameters within which technological options are assessed. The use of catalytic converters in cars does not address the generic problems of the internal combustion engine, nor does the substitution, for CFCs, of new chemicals in aerosol sprays address problems of pollution, or plastics disposal.

Finally, these techniques, when they reach the marketplace, are based on the idea of *individual*, rather than social, preference. From the point of view of market economies, the decision to consume rests with individuals, who at best can be coaxed or persuaded to act differently. (Much more commonly, however, individual consumer's preferences are built into the design of 'environmentally friendly' products). They represent a very fragile basis for changing public attitudes and instituting a thorough review of economic and social policy.

'Managerial' solutions to environmental problems, as they are presented to individuals in the developed, industrialised economies of the North, may be no more than cosmetic devices, which respond to public disquiet or taste. To some extent, environmental accounting techniques make environmental costs more *visible*, which can be desirable if, as a consequence, the political decisions implicit in given levels of consumption are not ignored. But such techniques are no substitute for these political decisions, and are useful only in as much as they facilitate difficult decision-making.

The uncomfortable doubt remains that environmental management might actually reinforce underlying imbalances in the way we source our consumption, and generate and dispose of wastes. If the underlying balance of sustainability is not changed, then what prospect is there that our 'getting and spending...' will be re-examined, and its consequences re-assessed? As we shall see, before effective action can be taken to curb unsustainable practices, we need to have a much clearer picture of *what makes unsustainable behaviour fully acceptable*. This is discussed in the next chapter.

DEMOCRATIC CONTROL OF THE ENVIRONMENT

The Earth Summit raised questions not only of what should be done to manage the global environment, but of how it should be done. This concern with participation in decision making is largely attributable to the enhanced role of the non-governmental organisations (NGOs). The Brundtland Commission had sought to foster links with voluntary bodies and private organisations involved in environmental activities, which lay outside the formal structure of government organisations. In many countries, NGOs were more important than government bodies in the environmental field, especially in developing countries where resources for environmental management were often limited. In Rio in 1992 the NGO meeting, the Global Forum, captured as much attention as the parallel inter-governmental meetings. These initiatives continued, even without wholehearted official backing, in the activities of the Commission for Sustainable Development.

The preparatory meetings for UNCED highlighted the importance of the NGOs, which in turn emphasised the need to mobilise popular support for environmental objectives. Sustainable development was considered a vacuous concept if it did not have the full support of the public. The increasing emphasis from official quarters on 'democratic' decision-making in global environmental management, is clear if we compare the first *World Conservation Strategy* published in 1983, with *Caring For The Earth* (WCS 1991), the second strategy published a decade later. Opinion-formation and political mobilisation are explicitly discussed in the later document. They have come to characterise much of the rhetoric, if not the reality, surrounding the UNCED process.

The second major element to shift attention towards the way global policy interventions might be managed, was the role of the World Bank, and particularly its Environment Department. During the 1970s and early 1980s the World Bank paid relatively little attention to environmental questions (Hall 1985). Environmental aspects of development funding were, on the whole, only considered after project approval was likely to be forthcoming, and only a small proportion of Bank-funded projects were submitted to rigorous project appraisal. This was partly because of the small number of Bank staff working in the environmental area, but also reflected deeper attitudes towards 'interference' from ecologically minded activists. Large-scale projects, such as the Papaloapan Basin in southern Mexico, had served to alienate both anthropologists and ecologists from large-scale development projects (Ewell and Poleman 1980).

During the 1980s, the World Bank gradually came to pay much more attention to environmental evaluation, hiring new staff and consultants of undoubted ability, such as Herman Daly and Norman Myers. In radical Green circles, this did little to guarantee sympathetic treatment of the Bank's activities. A number of issues of the influential journal *The Ecologist* scrutinised projects supported by the World Bank, while the environmental lobby of the United States Congress to withdraw Bank funding assumed much more importance.

The 'new' global agenda, around issues such as climate change, the destruction of tropical forests and biodiversity, together with the rights of indigenous people (an issue which the Bank had identified as sensitive at an early stage) attracted a high profile in the media generally. It was relatively easy to gain the support of environmental activists in the North in pressing these issues. There appeared to be few costs in taking preventative action, and most activists were unlikely to confront these problems face-to-face. Indeed, it can be plausibly argued that global campaigns about problems which were sufficiently distant, and which seemed to require few changes in the behaviour of individuals, were likely to be successful. The wearing of animal furs and the use of hardwoods were in no way essential to modern life. Changes in behaviour were not difficult to achieve, and bore few political costs.

Establishing more democratic control of environmental management in developing countries is more difficult the closer one is to the ground. Power is very unevenly distributed in most societies. In most poor countries, access to management tools for modifying the environmental impacts of development, is particularly unevenly distributed.

Many of the environmental management tools which have been developed, especially economic incentives, make little allowance for the powerlessness of the poor, their lack of information, and the vested interests of landlords and the military with which they contend. On the whole, wider public engagement with environmental rights, to land and to water, for example – including property rights – has been denied to the poor. On the contrary, conservation objectives have traditionally been imposed on local people, often from a basis in colonial history (Grove and Anderson 1987).

In addition, the effect of structural adjustment policies in the 1980s was to impose a new set of conditions on many poor people, especially in the poorest countries, which they were ill-equipped to deal with. There is considerable evidence that this served to undermine community solidarity, as the orientation to the market took precedence over traditional, and often sustainable, systems of cultivation.

The weakening of the public sector, too, while it may have diminished unnecessary bureaucracy, also removed some of the props essential to the livelihood of the poor. The key ingredient of successful environmental management at the local level is the power to make a significant difference to the outcome of policies. Many of the provisions agreed at UNCED require a level of public understanding and support at the local level, in both developed and developing countries, which in turn depends on public confidence in change. It is existing relations of power that limit environmental choices, and make for unsustainable development, not the absence of policy alternatives.

THE STANDARD OF LIVING OR THE QUALITY OF LIFE?

As we saw in Chapter Three, global levels of consumption continue to rise. We have already noted the inequalities to which this gives rise. Even the poorest fifth of the British population enjoys levels of consumption far higher than those enjoyed by the majority in the South. According to *Social Trends* in 1990/91 over 80 per cent of the poorest quintile in the UK had a television, freezer, washing machine and video recorder. Even some conveniences denied to manual workers' families twenty-five years ago, such as a telephone and central heating, were common among such families by 1993: over two-thirds of households possessed them (HMSO 1994).

How do these figures compare with the global situation? Table 6.1 divides the planet into three principal consumption classes: the relatively rich consumers who make up the majority in the North and

Table 6.1 Consumption classes: the global picture

Category of consumption	Consumers 1.1 billion	Middle 3.3 billion	Poor 1.1 billion
Diet	meat, processed food, soft drinks	grain, clean water	insufficient grain, dirty water
Transport	private cars	bicycles buses	walking
Materials	throw-aways	durables	local biomass
Status	'carnivores'	'omnivores'	'herbivores'
Commodities	replace	repair	re-use

Source: adapted freely from *World Watch Institute* (Durning 1992)

the elite in most of the South; the global majority, who are poor by developed country standards, but well above the subsistence threshold; and the one billion or so of the world's poorest people. There are a number of features of these global consumption classes that deserve attention:

1. The richer you are, the more likely it is that you eat processed, industrialised foods.
2. Personal mobility is closely linked to poverty: private transport is a prerogative of the relatively rich. This increased mobility is linked to enhance life-chances, and a greater ability to find employment outside the local area.
3. Particularly in rural areas, it is the poorest groups which are most dependent on the local biomass for their survival.

It is clear that the environmental implications of consumption are different for these different classes of consumers.

Disposing of waste products, especially consumer goods, is closely related to affluence. As income falls, people spend more time repairing their possessions; as income rises they tend to replace them. The trade-off here is one of time. The poor may not have more time, but they have less disposable income with which to trade time off against other factors, such as convenience and novelty. Gadgil and Guha (1995) refer to poor people in India, whose livelihoods are dependent on local resources, as 'ecosystem people' or 'herbivores'. Greater affluence enables individuals to draw resources from further away, a process which converts herbivores into omnivores and omnivores into carnivores. Ultimately, our conversion into 'carnivores' has less to do with meat-eating than with the value added by the food system (Goodman and Redclift 1991).

These patterns of consumption deliberately exaggerate the differences between global consumption classes, but if we are to 'think globally', such comparisons are valid. They are also reflected in the volume of materials consumed per capita, in the developed and developing countries. Comparative data show patterns of consumption which make very different demands of the resource base. Non-renewable materials, such as iron and steel, are disproportionately consumed by people in the North. In its original state, the same volume of wood is consumed by individuals in the South as in the North. One in four people shares a car, in the developed world, compared with one in a hundred in the developing countries Table 6.2).

Table 6.2 Comparative resource consumption, North and South (kg or m² per capita)

	Developed	**Developing**
Food: cereals	717	247
milk	320	39
meat	61	11
Wood: roundwood	388	339
sawn wood	213	19
paper	148	11
Fertilisers	70	15
Cement	451	130
Iron and steel	469	36
Aluminium	16	1
Cars	0.28	0.01

Source: Parikh 1991

The point about these comparisons is that they might lead us to question what is meant by the 'standard of living', since levels of consumption vary so dramatically, and what represents comfort and security in one setting implies deprivation in another. We might also reflect that the apparently mandatory increase in the standard of living in the North is linked to increasing volumes of disposable waste. One measure of increases in the 'standard of living', indeed, is the volume of household waste, and the increased costs associated with its disposal. We might reflect that, in this sense, improvements in the *standard* of life contribute, after a certain point (which was reached some time ago in the North) to a fall in the *quality* of life. We are still exhorted, most recently in the White Paper on Science and Technology in the United Kingdom, to seek wealth creation, 'and to improve the quality of Life' but the two objectives are not easily pursued together (OST 1993).

In addition to the mounting problems of waste disposal, associated with higher living standards in the North, is the question of energy production, which we considered in Chapter Three. Estimates of energy consumption for the United Kingdom are the basis for carbon dioxide emissions. In 1990, the United Kingdom emissions totalled 160 million tonnes of carbon. The figures for sources of carbon dioxide emissions exclude the use of electricity, by households, industry and agriculture, which are attributed to power stations. The figures for final energy consumer redistribute the contribution from power stations and refineries to the end consumer.

It is clear that assessing the costs of consumption is more than a book-keeping exercise. If we link carbon emissions to their end use, then responsibility falls squarely upon households and individual consumers. If we look at where energy is generated, much of it to produce electricity for the industrial and private consumer, then the problem of emissions can be located at the level of the state. As we saw in Chapter Five, as long as energy policy is developed without giving serious attention to environmental factors, the problem will remain. We know that energy efficiency is enhanced when the consumer is encouraged to make economies in end use, but in most countries people are actively encouraged to use more energy rather than less. Clearly other economies need to be made, towards combined heat and power generation, for example. But the allocation of responsibility for energy consumption is a vital part of any successful drive towards sustainable energy policies. Political choices might include better management of the demand for energy, *as well as* efficiencies in its end use. Better demand management would require a fundamental shift in the way consumer society organises itself and, at the same time, represent an advance on policies which take the level of production, and consumption, for granted.

The 'forcing factors', which increase consumption and feed our standard of living, are not confined to the industrial countries. The second *World Conservation Strategy* (WCS 1991) demonstrated that the planet has 42 countries in which energy consumption per capita is high, and which consume 80 per cent of the commercial energy generated. They accounted for only one quarter of the globe's population in 1991.

By contrast, the other 128 countries have relatively low levels of energy consumption per capita, and account for only 20 per cent of the energy consumed. These countries make up over three-quarters of the world's population. On average, someone in a high-consumption country consumes 18 times as much energy as someone in a low consumption country. The average citizen of the United States consumes five times as much energy as a citizen of Mexico, and over one hundred times as much energy as somebody in Bangladesh (WCS 1991, Annex 5).

These inequalities in energy consumption are matched by those of waste disposal. The World Bank's *World Development Report* of 1992 (IBRD 1992) showed that Singapore and Hong Kong dispose of as much toxic wastes as the whole of sub-Saharan Africa (O'Keefe et al 1993). At the same time it is important to recognise that most global sinks are located in the less developed countries where the 'costs' of disposal – including the value of the poor's labour – are much lower! This provides an excellent example of the trap into which we can fall: poverty, by contributing to fewer wastes, can absorb the costs of their disposal more 'cheaply'. Disposing of waste is a distributive issue, as is the creation of waste and the provision of sink functions, at the global level. To begin to achieve sustainable development we need to address issues of poverty and equity from within a global perspective. This the UNCED process has failed to do. Alternative ways of representing these distributive questions can be demonstrated through the use of international carbon budgets.

GLOBAL CARBON BUDGETS

The Earth Summit at Rio made a number of things clear. It was evident that the ability to reach agreements to curb atmospheric emissions of greenhouse gasses turned on the question of responsibility. The developing countries held very different convictions about responsibility for global warming from the countries of the North. In the view of the South, the industrialised world bore responsibility for the historical situation, since Europe and North America had industrialised first. The accumulation of greenhouse gasses during the last century was principally the responsibility of the North.

There were also wide differences of opinion about the units of assessment for greenhouse gas emissions. The less developed countries argue that assessment should be based on per capita emissions, counting an Indian peasant farmer in the same way as an American executive. This kind of calculation would lay the burden of responsibility, current and historical, at the feet of the North. But there were other issues of significance, too. Should we equate the emission of gases such as methane, produced from paddy-fields and by animal ruminants, so-called 'livelihood emissions', with the emissions from the exhaust of the European, Japanese or North American car?

One of the most contested areas at UNCED, and subsequently, has been the role of sinks in sequestering carbon from the atmosphere. Initially, the World Resources Institute in Washington produced a set of calculations, which appeared to demonstrate that responsibility for both emissions, and their absorption (in sinks), was roughly equally divided between the industrialised and non-industrialised world (WRI 1991). This suggestion was important, of course, to the negotiating position of the United States and other industrialised countries in Rio. However, the evidence adduced by the World Resources Institute was heavily contested by a number of organisations and individuals in the South, notably Anil Agarwal of the Centre for Science and Environment in Delhi. Agarwal, and his colleague Narain, argued that the World Resource Institute figures had been based on some major misconceptions and biases. Essentially, these figures placed too much credibility on projections for economic growth in the South, took unrepresentative years for tropical deforestation in the Amazon, and dealt with both CFCs and methane in a highly tendentious way (Agarwal and Narain 1991) (See Figure 6.2).

In the context of these discussions, and other documentary information from developing countries themselves, it has proved difficult to reach agreement on the underlying issue of responsibility for any anticipated global warming. Attempts by the North to link better environmental management to overseas aid ('Green conditionality') are strongly resisted in the South. Progress at reaching targets for emission levels at the national level has been slow, although it has been assisted by economic recession in Europe. Reaching global targets is quite another matter. Even the kinds of modest policy initiatives which might enable countries to achieve workable global targets, such as tradeable permits for emissions, are unpopular with most Northern governments. From a Southern point of view, meeting global targets without such mechanisms looks like imposing the

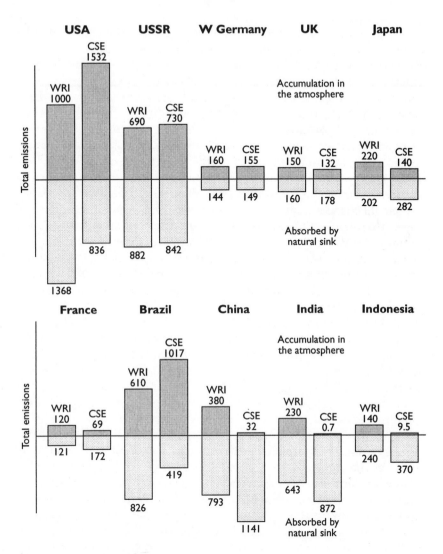

Source: Agarwal and Narain 1991

Figure 6.2 Comparative values of greenhouse gas emissions of WRI's top
ten emitting nations (in million tonnes of carbon equivalent)

Northern agenda for climate change on the poorer countries of the
South.

As we saw in Chapter Four, the minimum condition for reaching
agreement about the measures that need to be taken at the global

level is to address the quality of development, enabling the developing countries (including those like the Asian 'tigers') to make the transition towards lower energy intensity. This would not remove the threat of global warming, but it would reduce it.

The feasibility of a lower energy-intensity transition, in which developing countries have better access to cleaner technologies and the developed countries decommission their existing plant, depends upon the benefits being spelt out clearly. At the moment, as we have seen, environmental regulation tends to benefit the industrialised countries, where companies can see clear market advantages in cleaner production and associated marketing. The increased industrial competitiveness of large multinational companies, located in the North, is not difficult to marry with the containment of climate change. It is not a very significant step in achieving sustainable development at the global level, however, especially if the costs of cleaner production in the North are passed to the countries of the South. At the heart of the debate surrounding sustainable development is the vexed question of current levels of investment in production and consumption, and the extent to which these are sustainable. Ecological modernisation, I would suggest, is not a solution to sustainable development globally, but even retreading capital investment in this way has insufficient political support in the North.

In the view of some economists, another method for measuring (and therefore, potentially, equalising) the global balance sheet, is to take carbon budgets as a point of departure. The important thing about carbon budgets is that they are based upon our capacity to 'manage' our levels of carbon emission, as the basis of changing the allocation of resources between North and South. In other words, the use of carbon budgets would help establish the level of wastes, and the role of carbon sinks, as part of an alternative assessment of what could make development 'sustainable'. Table 6.3, taken from *Energy Policy In The Greenhouse* (Krause et al 1990), shows how we might begin to make an assessment of the 'breathing space' that we are allowed by stabilising current levels of emission.

It is possible to calculate the contribution of individual countries to this carbon ceiling on the basis of their populations, and to calculate further the number of years it will take before they meet their budgeted carbon total. Some countries will have to make the shift towards reduced emissions much more quickly than others. If the developed world took seriously the challenge of global warming, and the primary responsibility which it bears for the problem, some

Table 6.3 How quickly must fossil fuels be phased out?

	1986 Release rate (tons/cap-yr[1])	Percentage of IC average	1985–2100 Fossil carbon allowance[2] (btC)	Years left at 1986 release rates
Portugal	0.79	23	1.26	155
Spain	1.28	38	4.78	96
Yugoslavia	1.49	44	2.88	83
Greece	1.62	47	1.23	77
New Zealand	1.63	48	0.41	75
Italy	1.65	49	7.06	74
Israel	1.68	49	0.53	73
Switzerland	1.79	53	0.80	70
France	1.79	53	6.84	70
Austria	1.93	57	0.94	65
Sweden	1.95	57	1.04	64
Iceland	1.97	58	0.03	62
Hungary	1.98	58	1.31	62
Japan	2.11	62	14.99	59
Norway	2.14	63	0.52	58
Ireland	2.15	63	0.44	57
Romania	2.41	71	2.83	51
Netherlands	2.41	71	1.80	51
Belgium	2.68	79	1.22	46
South Africa	2.78	82	3.99	43
UK	2.94	86	7.00	42
Finland	3.02	89	0.60	41
FR Germany	3.07	90	7.51	40
Poland	3.32	97	4.63	37
Denmark	3.34	98	0.63	37
USSR	3.59	105	34.69	34
Bulgaria	3.60	106	1.11	34
Australia	3.85	113	1.97	32
Canada	4.09	120	3.16	30
Czechoslovakia	4.21	124	1.91	29
USA	5.01	147	29.81	25
German DR	5.50	161	2.05	22
Luxembourg	6.42	188	0.05	19
Total IC average	*3.22*	*100*	*150.00*	*47*

Notes: IC – industrialised country

1 1986 release rates from Marland et al (1988), including cement.
2 Allocation shares calculated on the basis of 1986 UN population data.

Source: Krause et al 1990

form of modified carbon budgeting might offer important bench-marks. It would then be a matter of devising policies, such as a carbon tax or tradeable permits, to enable individual countries to reach their targeted emission levels. This would represent an enormous stride towards global environmental management.

Global carbon budgets would provide an opportunity to make a realistic assessment of the implications of current economic growth, and associated levels of consumption, of the way we use resources and sinks. It should be emphasised, of course, that such budgets are tools for sustainable development, not a substitute for policies.

At the moment, the attention of most Northern governments is on the costs of using resources more sustainably, in terms of the effects of more sustainable production on current economic activities. If, instead, we focused on the costs of existing practices, and sought to bring levels of consumption into line with the 'externalities' of economic growth, we might begin to formulate scenarios for effective transitions out of current energy-wasteful and polluting development. We would begin, as it were, with the consequences of our actions, and read backwards towards the more sustainable levels of consumption and production. The key concept with which to embark on this process is the way we have chosen to metabolise nature and its global implications. Our management of the environment would at last address the process of development, rather than its more intractable outcomes.

To make this exercise credible we need to do a number of things. First, we need to develop a realistic political economy of sinks, as well as sources, of greenhouse gases and other waste materials. Second, we need to explore the ways in which a better grip on our meta-bolisation of nature can be translated into a workable economic and social programme, which is understood and endorsed by civil society, not just in the North, but in the South, too.

These are policy objectives that carry massive implications for the research we do into the relationship between development and the environment. They are Utopian only in the sense that they require political vision, as well as better management. The opportunity exists to make environmental management our servant, rather than our master. The effective use of management tools, like carbon budgets, would need to be preceded by a radical shift in global political thinking.

THE SOCIAL FUNCTIONS OF SINKS

If environmental management is to follow from radical changes in global development, rather than act as a substitute for such changes, we might begin with the role of global sinks.

Behind much of the political rhetoric about global environmental change lies an uncomfortable fact: we know relatively little about how global sinks work. Much of the background discussion about responsibility for global warming, and the conservation of bio-diversity, rests on a poor understanding of the part played by sinks in the carbon balance. This is clear, for example, from the widely different estimates of carbon emissions, and the part played by sinks in carbon sequestration, which were put forward by the World Resources Institute, in Washington, and the Centre for Science and Environment in Delhi (see Table 5.4). Discussion of the competing claims of these organisations reflects substantially different approaches to sink functions, as well as divergent arithmetic.

Uncertainty surrounds much of the physical science of the carbon cycle, particularly the role of the oceans. It is not surprising, then, that human responsibilities for the way sinks are managed, and destroyed, remain heavily contested. Uncertain science has acted as a cover for political inadequacies. A better grasp of the social functions of sinks might usefully inform the parties to international agreements, but it will need to extend beyond the current theories of value, both neo-classical and Marxist, whose intellectual ancestry was forged by the needs of hydrocarbon society.

As we saw in Chapter Three, most emissions to air and water, as well as the solid wastes produced through economic activity, are what process engineers call 'environmental burdens'. In the language of materials systems they are also referred to, interestingly, as 'dissip-ative losses'. They do not contribute to the maintenance of the system: they are externalised, and placed at a distance. As Connett has observed, the language of waste reflects our human concerns with particular precision, whether it is couched in scientific credibility, or the vernacular of everyday life (Connett 1993, 101).

Sinks are repositories for these emissions and wastes but, as we have seen, they are rarely the final repositories. For example, 'recycling' of chemical batteries continues in landfills, when they are dumped unceremoniously together with other domestic rubbish. As Robert Ayres notes, 'the industrial system does not generally recycle its nutrients' (Ayres 1994, 5). At the same time, of course, anthropo-genic emissions of carbon are only a relatively small part of the total picture. The full story of the carbon cycle suggests that fluctuations in carbon emissions from human activity, although perhaps critical for the human-induced greenhouse effect, are relatively minor in terms of the biological time-frame (Krause et al 1990).

Nevertheless, the existence of carbon sinks, at the global level, may be important in reducing net emissions of carbon from human activities. In 1990 the Intergovernmental Panel on Climate Change (IPCC) estimated fossil fuel emissions at 5.4 billion tonnes, while 1.6 billion tonnes of carbon were attributed to deforestation, that is, the reduced carbon storage that resulted from forest losses. Most policies to redress this shortfall, using economic instruments, are unlikely to make very much difference. For example, it has been suggested that private capital could be mobilised to help fund forest conservation, setting new afforestation projects against carbon emission levels. Countries that wanted to reduce their carbon emissions could therefore do so through carbon offsets rather than reductions in emission levels. Protecting more trees in other countries, or growing more in your own, might be a more acceptable basis for global agreements than the difficult task of simply limiting levels of emission.

However, a study of the role of international carbon offsets concludes that such a policy is probably not feasible because of difficulties in monitoring, enforcement and 'the implicit change in property rights involved in "selling" carbon sequestration rights' (Brown and Adger 1993, 20). Such carbon offsets have more potential on a bilateral basis, between countries. However, even here it is not clear that the Climate Change Convention would 'allow the enhancement of sinks made as a result of bilateral agreements to count as part of the donating country's inventory' (Brown and Adger 1993, 8).

To invoke sinks as a positive factor in negotiations implies changes in the way we acknowledge property rights. The North would be seen as 'buying forest' from the South, where countries would be seen as implicitly giving up part of their property rights to their own resources. Again, it is difficult to foresee improvements in the management of the global environment, without major changes in economic thinking and practice.

Our interference with the environment, an essential part of the human economic activity, draws together two increasingly incompatible models, one from nature, and the other one from the governing economic ideology. The First and Second Laws of Thermodynamics state that matter and energy can neither be created nor destroyed, but simply converted from one form into another. These are the 'closed' systems that have been referred to throughout this discussion. It follows that any value they acquire during this process of conversion (including, of course, the production of commodities and services for human use) is governed by *human* laws rather than physical ones. As Ayres puts it, 'the economic system is, in essence, the metabolic regulatory system' (Ayres 1994, 4).

The costs of industrial societies' metabolism are increasingly being shifted from the terrestrial system to that of the atmosphere (Fischer-Kowalski and Haberl 1993). The prospect of global warming demonstrates the impossibility of managing biospheric systems with economic tools designed for allocating scarce resources and producing commodities, on the basis of capitalist, market, principles.

This is not to say that we cannot place a value upon nature. A 'value' can be placed on carbon sequestration, as on any other process amenable to human interference. As we appreciate its importance for human economic activities, increased efforts will undoubtedly be made to attach market values in this way. However, we still need to ask whether attaching such values to the environment really addresses the underlying processes through which sinks assume value in the first place. Because sinks are regarded as essential to human economic activities they are viewed as a natural process. Their naturalisation is the outcome of an economic ideology that places production, and the pursuit of higher material standards for a minority, above sustainable livelihoods for the global majority. We need to consider not only the role that sinks play in natural systems, but the way they are naturalised in the first place. We need to turn our attention to the social processes that determine how we manage the environment.

Chapter Seven
Sustainability and Social Commitments

Within the context of environmental management, the environment is usually understood in terms of the functions it performs. Any discussion of the way our consumption transforms the environment therefore needs to begin with the uses to which it is put. In this chapter we will explore the way in which environmental management is undertaken, the institutionalised practices through which the environment is managed, and the assumptions, or discourses, surrounding the environment.

The social practices that themselves lead to these environmental functions, our underlying social commitments, are frequently ignored. Considered against the background of the way we metabolise nature, discussed in the previous chapter, it is argued that sustainability will prove elusive unless we explore the potential, not simply of environmental management tools, but of the institutional practices that give rise to them.

Figure 7.1 provides a model of the way that human societies make use of the environment. There are three principal functions: taking, adding and replacing. (This model is adapted freely from Redclift and Woodgate 1993, and draws on Catton and Dunlap 1993.) These environmental uses are related to economic activities which themselves reflect human social purposes, the 'getting and spending' that characterises modern complex societies.

ENVIRONMENT

Taking	Adding	Replacing
Ozone hole Overfishing Deforestation Soil erosion Whaling Mining Species extinction	Acid rain Acid pollution Radiation Global warming Pesticides Nitrates Sewage Waste disposal Population	Habitats Drainage Urbanisation Conifer plantations Environmental knowledge

ENVIRONMENTAL USES

1. SUPPLY DEPOT → FINITE RESOURCES/LIMITS TO GROWTH (TAKING)
2. WASTE REPOSITORY → POLLUTION → EXTERNALITIES   (ADDING)
3. LIVING SPACE → AMENITY AND LIVELIHOOD   (REPLACING)
            (NORTH)   (SOUTH)

ENVIRONMENTAL MANAGEMENT

Source: adapted from Redclift and Woodgate 1993, with reference to Dunlop (1993)

Figure 7.1 A model of human use of the environment

In this model, taking from the environment, for example, for fishing, forestry or mining, means that the environment serves as a supply depot. In the second case we are adding to the environment, through pollution or the increased consumption associated with increased population. The environment is serving as a waste repository. In the third case, that of 'replacing', the environment is acting as a living space, as a source of amenity and livelihood.

In essence, environmental management is concerned with managing the contradictions inherent in combining the uses to which the environment is put. Sometimes using the environment to perform two or more of these functions implies a supplementary relationship. For example, using a reservoir for fishing might have no adverse effect on its value for electricity generation. Indeed the two activities might be complementary. On other occasions, however, different environmental uses imply a competitive relationship. Increasing the utility derived from one use of the environment may reduce the utility derived from another. For example, if we were to use the reservoir for water sports, such as power boating, this would almost certainly have an adverse effect on the area's potential as a nature reserve. One way of regarding environmental management, then, is to see it as a way of matching the supply functions of the environment against the other functions it performs (Redclift and Woodgate 1993). Within modern industrial society the object of environmental management is to ensure the flows of natural resources needed for economic growth, without prejudicing the maintenance and enhancement of natural capital stocks (Pearce 1991).

Consideration of the environment's sink functions is secondary: they are only considered when there is a recognisable threat, for example, through sewage or air pollution, to human health or the maintenance of the environment's supply function. Some sink functions might also represent a disturbance in the amenity value of the environment. The social commitments which drive our patterns of consumption, and recreation, are not normally themselves subject to environmental policy intervention. Altering these practices might enhance overall environmental sustainability, as we shall see, but it represents a deeper level of political responsibility that is not part of most political discourse today.

In a sense this model of environmental uses is functionalist, in that the definition of human purposes towards the environment is given by existing social commitments, which are not questioned. We have also established that management practices to resolve competitive uses for the environment are based on implicit social priorities. In most cases, for example, the extraction of mineral resources (or, indeed, the disposal of waste from existing production processes) and the needs of economic growth receive priority over the preservation of ecosystems, or of individual species. It is indicative that our attention is drawn to ecosystems and species, on the whole, precisely when they are most under threat. Environmental management is a reactive, responsive mode of intervention.

ENVIRONMENTAL DISCOURSE AND ENVIRONMENTAL MANAGEMENT

It is an axiom that we can only know about nature through our discourse about it. What is often missed, however, is that environmental management represents one discourse, among several, about nature. It represents nature as existing separately from us, as performing functions for us. As we have seen, this discourse is based on assumptions about the way we use the environment, particularly our consumption habits which are not themselves explored in the context of policy choices. The question is then: do existing practices leave us confident that we can arrive at other discourses about the environment? Would other discourses lead us to a different understanding of the environment, and what would they imply for our actions?

Writing about Edward Lorenz's first faltering steps towards what has come to be known as chaos theory, Gleich has sketched out some of the biases within science, or rather, within professional scientific discourse. Science is beset with specialisms, and with the need to advance its own authority. This frequently leads to claims for scientific uncertainty, or the suppression of uncertainty, rather than an admission that there are different ways of arriving at the truth:

> Few laymen realized how tightly compartmentalised the scientific community had become, a battleship sealed against leaks.

> (Gleich 1987, 31)

As we shall see, there are enormous challenges to the way we understand the environment from the plural rationalities that are reflected in simultaneous discourses. Some social sciences, notably economics, instead seek to acquire increased legitimacy from emulating the methods of the natural sciences, aspiring to be a global social science. In this respect, neoclassical economics exemplifies the idea of displacement, by forming a view of the environment which is dictated by science (scientific knowledge) rather than culture.

In assessing our capacity to fully understand the forces which drive our use of the environment, especially our habitual levels of consumption, we need to explore the way that intellectual biases in the policy sciences inhibit our room for manoeuvre.

Underlying the question of uncertainty, which characterises environmental issues, is a basic confusion. This is the confusion between the limitations in what we know about nature (scientific facts) and the limitations of the science, with which we explore and understand nature. Increasingly, the social sciences are in the front line of policy demands over the environment. They are expected to play their part in reducing the indeterminacy surrounding our knowledge of the environment. They are exhorted to produce more 'facts'.

What is seldom recognised, however, is that the models that are used to manage our relationship with the environment are themselves the product of a discourse, which is itself, inherently, ideological. By employing models of human interaction with the environment we are accessing not simply environmental knowledge, but knowledge (and discourse) about human behaviour. When we seek to practice environmental management, we are revealing aspects of our culture, and the 'objectivity' we claim is itself a cultural icon which we are in no position to be objective about.

This can be illustrated by considering some of the biases within the dominant model of environmental management, which we can call that of the 'rational individual calculator'. Economic frameworks and methods are founded upon a priori assumptions about human nature and social relations. Within the neoclassical economic paradigm, these suggest that the market is an efficient means of allocating resources and rewarding effort. As Gleich puts it:

> Modern economics relies heavily on the efficient market theory. Knowledge is assumed to flow freely from place to place. The people making important decisions are supposed to have access to more or less the same body of information...on the whole, once knowledge is public, economists assume that it is known everywhere
>
> (Gleich 1987, 181)

There are a number of aspects to this model which deserve close attention. According to this model, social interaction is only instrumental, in that it is designed to maximise utility for the individual. Social interaction is not considered as constituting value in its own right, because the behaviour of human beings has no intrinsic value, independent of the needs they express in the market. In this view the tastes and preferences of individuals are considered as given, and enquiring into their origins is not considered part of the business of being an economist. In the language of Manfred Max-

Neef people are 'object persons' rather than 'subject persons' (Max-Neef in 1991). They exist, for neoclassical economics, through their stated preferences, as expressed in market prices.

This model has a number of implications for what has already been written about the way we metabolise the environment, and our difficulty in managing the consequences of this process. As it is, our underlying social commitments, the behaviour which determines the way resources are transformed, are excluded from environmental policy interventions.

There are a number of problems with the conventional economic model as we have characterised it. First, there is very little room in such an analysis for genuinely social experience. In a sense, the neoclassical model reduces society to the sum of the individuals constituting it. The more we learn about changing habits of consumption in the eighteenth and nineteenth centuries, the more important the role of consumption goods as a means of intensifying family values and transmitting status (Brewer and Porter 1993). The way that individuals 'consume' reflects the way that society values consumption. Consumption behaviour is an effect as well as a cause.

Second, the idea of rational, calculating individuals, as a key to understanding economic behaviour, imposes one model of human behaviour, and reifies one definition of rationality over other definitions. It also assumes a good deal about calculation, by reducing human behaviour to the achievement of individual goals.

Third, this model is ethnocentric, in that it imposes one cultural vision on all others regardless of their unique basis in values. This is quite consistent with the globalising intentions of economics as a discipline. If human beings, like nature, have intrinsic value, such value is hidden behind the value they assume as consumers, producers or customers. It is clear that when we talk about the environment as a resource, we are, effectively, talking about how we ourselves value nature primarily for what it can produce. We are conferring upon nature the unproblematic functional role that we regularly confer upon ourselves in the marketplace.

Models of human behaviour are based on social values, prior social commitments, which we enter into as members of society, and which themselves enable us to generate our models. An important feature of environmental management, in which neoclassical analysis plays such a central part, is the way that human purposes are read into the environment. This can be illustrated by the way the environment is referred to as if it is an instrumental resource: the North Sea is a 'waste sink', tropical forests are 'carbon sinks', and so on. To achieve this perspective on the environment, of course, we need to be distanced from it, it needs to be objectified and apparently removed from human purposes. However, as I have argued already, environmental management's delineation of objective functions in the environment is more apparent than real, since social commitments are already built into the model, and the use to which it is put.

If we are to assume more responsibility for the underlying causes of environmental problems, then it may be worth exploring alternative models of human behaviour, which seek to establish different relationships with the environment. It is an indication of our collective inability to act to reverse environmental degradation that 'nature' has come to assume its present importance. Our appreciation of nature increases with its scarcity value. The environment seems to assume most importance, in global terms, when sustainability is placed in jeopardy, and environmental knowledge is being lost.

Many of the social objectives which reflect environmental knowledge, and make the environment a contested domain, especially in the South, are part of a critical perspective which does not fit with conventional wisdom about economic growth and development. Much of this knowledge is the repository of non-experts and non-formal institutions. It lies in everyday behaviour and cultures which are not based upon 'objective' knowledge. Rather than attempt to reduce behaviour to the economic terms that are comprehensible within a neoclassical paradigm, we might examine the circumstances under which environmental management, as a policy exercise, is contested. We will then need to formulate existing environmental knowledge in different ways, to reflect both its intended consequences and those which fit awkwardly with other knowledges.

Issues such as global climate change are often presented as if what is at stake is the credibility of the scientific community. The importance of the time frame, within which evidence will be adduced 'for' or 'against' global warming, is interpreted as central to the survival of science. Global problems require improved climate modelling, and elicit calls for more facts about what is likely to happen to global climate. On the basis of these facts, it is held, we will be better placed to act in the face of future uncertainties.

Such an account does not make it clear how we determine when we are in possession of enough information to make a rational judgement. Our willingness to shape new policy responses is more likely to be determined by the discovery of new technological opportunities, and the anticipated political costs, than by achieving a level of factual knowledge equal to the task.

Environmental management is heavily dependent on regulatory action, including science and technology policy, which constantly changes the problem we are witnessing, and seeking to understand. Many of the environmental problems with which we have become familiar, especially at the global level, such as the disposal of toxic wastes, air pollution and the destruction of ecosystems in the tropics, are themselves outcomes of the application of science and technology to definable 'human' problems. It would be surprising, then, if policies to redress damage to the environment were free from political judgements.

In the face of increased uncertainty we need to confront a far more radical prospect. This is that our social practices themselves have become so institutionalised that we need to look outside formal science for answers to many of the problems that face us. Our underlying social commitments are bound up with everyday life, in the industrialised world, and manifested in a host of different ways, that need to be examined. For example, the right to individual motorised mobility is enshrined in the way we regard the motor car. Challenging this commitment may mean redefining the relationship between where we live and where we work. It will require an altogether more radical way of 'managing' the environment.

As we have already seen, in Chapter Three, our increased use of fossil-fuel energy is another commitment which is central to our economies, as well as the economic logic we have developed. An examination of our commitments might begin by exploring the environmental costs of energy conversion, and the market value we attach to commodities which require high levels of energy for their production. These commitments, in turn, are driven by what often appear as almost existential goals, which are usually taken for granted, like a higher standard of living or increased leisure time.

The preoccupation with the environment in policy discourse in the developed economies, is often viewed as evidence of a cultural shift in attitudes, from which there is no escape. We are entering, on this account, a new environmental age.

However, a rather different interpretation could be placed on public concern with the environment. Governments and policymakers (the term 'policymaker' itself expresses this relationship) usually react to environmental problems, many of them produced by science and technology, in order to maintain their own authority. In the process they frequently seek to develop, or manipulate, a social consensus around issues, largely by disputing the facts of the environmentalist case. It is clear that public apprehension about the environment is itself a symptom of the neglect of environmental issues in the way that other economic and social policies are framed. Once again, the attachment of an 'environmental' label to problems provides a means of side-stepping underlying questions of sustainability. It enables us to draw a discrete veil over the choices we make in everyday life.

HOW WE METABOLISE NATURE

This chapter has examined the way that our social commitments are established, and the role of environmental management in seeking to modify them. It has examined the behaviour which gives rise to environmental problems. These are the institutional practices through which we extend our control over the environment, in terms of both accessing natural resources and disposing of wastes.

It has already been asserted that we lack a theoretical understanding of sink functions, matching that of resources. Theories of resource-use examine the means by which people in one part of the globe exploit resources located in another. Neoclassical economics speaks of the 'comparative advantage' through which different countries assume different roles in the international division of labour. The industrialised world traditionally looked to the South to source much of its raw materials for manufacturing, and for food. The developing countries, in turn, imported the manufactured goods produced in the North, in return for primary commodities and labour. A Marxist interpretation of the same relationships views imperialism as the mechanism through which developing countries are exploited, deriving their economic identity from their dependence on the industrialised world.

The territorial dimensions of resource-use have, understandably, been uppermost in the minds of those critical of the development process. As we saw in Chapter Six, Gadgil and Guha, in their analysis of the links between India's economic development and its environmental problems, distinguish between what they call 'omnivores' and 'herbivores' (Gadgil and Guha 1995). Omnivores are the beneficiaries of development in India, because they are able to live at one remove from the resources they exploit, which are frequently located at a considerable distance from them. This is doubly true, of course, of the majority of consumers in the North, whose goods and commodities utilise raw materials and labour from the South.

Herbivores, or 'ecosystem people' as Gadgil and Guha describe them, live closer to the resources they exploit and, as a consequence are affected by the changes wrought in the ecosystems from which the resources are derived. Herbivores do not necessarily act more sustainably, especially if they exist at the threshold of survival, but they do need to consider the effects of their behaviour on future generations of their own people. There is no built-in potential for similar sustainability in the case of herbivores, whose behaviour, as we have seen, is dictated by underlying commitments which pay little attention to the combined effect of patterns of consumption on other people's environments.

One recent development of this train of thought is the concern with 'ecological footprints', the impacts of Northern development on the developing world. Such footprints illustrate the 'rights and wrongs of extraterritorial action' in the words of the International Institute for Environment and Development (IIED 1992). The environment in the South is not a *tabula rasa*, or a black box into which we have put our economic system, but the result of continuing economic and political relations with the North. The issues surrounding development, such as trade liberalisation and the impacts of structural adjustment policies, serve to modify the footprints left by past generations.

It has been argued that the metabolisation of nature involves both the sourcing of development, as natural resources are drawn into the ambit of the market, and the utilisation of sinks, as wastes are returned to the environment. Clearly, sinks have a territorial dimension, too, and just as sourcing leaves ecological footprints in its wake, so does the creation of sinks. We have also noted that within an economy, as with biological systems, some units act in ways that are predatory or parasitical to others. It would be surprising if the creation of sinks, at the global territorial level, was achieved any more harmoniously than the creation of plantation systems or *entrepots*. In fact we have probably given even less attention to the effects of disposing of our wastes than we have to the procurement of raw materials.

There is another aspect of the way that development metabolises nature which deserves close attention, since it represents an important departure from traditional practices in the industrialised world. This is the way in which the environment is being transformed through intellectual property rights, and systems of information and knowledge, as well as through spatial control. Nature has become a human 'invention', capable of being patented like any other commodity.

The development of sophisticated computer systems, and the ability to genetically engineer 'natural' forms, outside a given habitat, have served to introduce new mechanisms of ownership and control.

The metabolisation of nature is no longer confined to geographically located systems of resources, but includes the knowledge base, and rights to property that exist in law, but can be removed from one location, or introduced into another. Individual countries, in particular, are usually unwilling to forfeit these rights. As Brown and Adger (1993) demonstrate, multilateral forest offsets, which would enable countries to augment their carbon budgets through helping to conserve forests elsewhere, necessarily interfere with the property rights of other states. They raise questions about the property value of sinks, of places where the right to exploit resources is becoming a matter of national sovereignty. The patenting of these rights is linked to the conservation of species, and entire ecosystems, providing an environmental dimension that scarcely existed a generation ago.

It is not an accident that the metabolisation of nature has assumed so much importance in recent years. It is bound up with the process of globalisation itself. Increasing importance is attached to what lies outside the globe, the extra-terrestrial environment, the Earth's atmosphere, as a sink for airborne matter. We might characterise environmental problems today as increasingly bound up with the atmosphere, as terrestrial colonisation (in the form of forests, the deep oceans and river basins, for example) fails to keep pace with the demands which we place upon the environment. Non-territorial space is becoming, literally, the location for global environmental problems.

These two dimensions are related, and present themselves in ways which our theories of resources and waste do not encompass. Environmental dangers are highlighted through resource conservation policies, such as debt-for-nature swaps, and forest offsets, but the underlying processes which have increased the importance of carbon sequestration are often ignored. They include the economic activities and social institutions behind the build-up of greenhouse gases in the atmosphere, and the failure to make substantial reductions in our dependence on fossil fuels. At the same time, intelligence about tropical forests, as well as about ways of engineering genetically modified organisms, is available through satellite monitoring, and computer simulations. We are in a better position to 'know' about the consequences of our consumption, without being willing to build environmental consequences into our everyday choices. The ingredients of the non-territorial environment enter into the financial calculations of multinational companies, whose shares are quoted on the Stock Exchange, but the environmental practices of these companies are often kept secret.

To develop a satisfactory theory of the way we metabolise nature, as we have seen, we need to examine issues such as the financial trade in waste, and the effect of sink conservation policies, such as debt-for-nature arrangements. We also need to explore the social practices which reduce the visibility of sinks, and which place them at a distance. These practices, like most environmental phenomena, are associated with high levels of uncertainty, as well as a good deal of ignorance. The mechanics of waste disposal, at the global level, are complex.

Environmental economists are increasingly interested in the costs of disposing of waste, as well as the costs of procuring resources. These costs are not part of the formal trading system, although efforts are being made to reform the system of international trading to reflect them. But it is also clear that there is an epistemological dimension to the social visibility of sinks, which we ignore at our peril. Michael Thompson reminds us that 'waste' is the quality conferred on a material by society, while 'management' is the social process through which it is institutionalised (Thompson 1990). We can begin to examine the social mechanisms through which our management of the environment is made 'natural', by considering the importance of language in the discourse upon nature. This will lead us to consider processes such as embodiment and distanciation.

EMBODIMENT AND DISTANCIATION

The language we use to describe them provides an indication of the value we attach to wastes. As Connett observes, we express our devaluation of waste in a routinised way, through the words we use. Words such as 'rubbish' and 'trash', not only describe the physical properties of waste, they have also entered our language as expletives (Connett 1990, 101).

The way in which we regard the waste products of human activities echoes organic waste: the detritus of organic systems. Brimblecombe, writing about air pollution, seeks to put this within an historical context. He argues that as our reverence for nature increased, with the spread of cities and industrialisation, so 'pollution' ceased to mean 'defilement' and began to take on a more secular resonance. Pollution had referred to ungodly activities, which were 'dirty'. Nature, in contrast, referred to deification and 'cleanliness' (Brimblecombe 1990, 100). It was the early nineteenth century Romantics who, in Brimblecombe's view, drew attention to the way in which we despoiled nature. In his view they took pollution from the human sphere, and placed it within the sphere of 'nature', to emphasise and contrast it against the 'natural' (and therefore godly).

The concepts of embodiment and distanciation help us to explore the relationship between the processes that occur 'out there' in the physical world, and those which lie in the socially generated realm of value (Thompson 1990, 117). Language mediates these two worlds, expressing the value judgements which underpin routinised economic and social processes.

At this point it may be useful to turn to Pierre Bourdieu, who has sought to explain the cultural processes that we take for granted (Bourdieu 1977). In his *Outline of a Theory of Practice*, Bourdieu argues that bodies of ideas develop around existing practices, as well as serving to anticipate alternatives. For this reason, practices are unlike ideologies, which we have to learn to know. Practices, according to Bourdieu, are *embodied* in ways which make them particularly powerful. They are part of the 'doxic' experience of the social world, which does not call attention to itself, but remains undisputed, and taken for granted.

Bourdieu compares two kinds of knowledge: phenomenological and objectivist. Phenomenological knowledge is an exploration of the familiar in unfamiliar terms:

> [it] sets out to make explicit the truth of primary experience of the social world, that is, all that is inscribed in the relationship of *familiarity* with the familiar environment, the unquestioning apprehension of the social world which, by definition, does not reflect on itself, and excludes the question of the conditions of its own proximity.
>
> (Bourdieu 1977, 3)

By contrast, objectivist knowledge consists of:

> tacitly assumed presuppositions [which] give the social world its self-evident, natural character.
>
> (Bourdieu 1977, 3)

Figure 7.2 represents the universe of discourse, of phenomenological knowledge, as the shaded area. This is the domain in which argument occurs, and opinions are formed. The unshaded area is the 'universe of the undiscussed' and undisputed, that which is taken for granted,

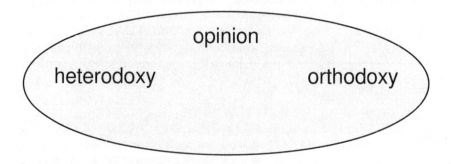

doxa: that which is taken for granted

opinion

heterodoxy

orthodoxy

Figure 7.2 The universe of the undiscussed

or 'doxa'. Everyday knowledge enters into human practices, it is part of the *doxic* experience of the social world. However, at certain times this knowledge is challenged; its familiarity is called into question through challenges to orthodoxy. The 'naturalness' of opinions is subjected to scrutiny, and frequently found wanting. Naturalisation of the social world, which necessarily excludes any consideration of the conditions that make an experience possible, is turned on its head.

Bourdieu argues that societies reach points of crisis when the embodied values that hold people together are forced apart:

> The critique which brings the undiscussed into discussion, the unformulated into formulation, has as the conditions of its possibility, objective crisis, which, in breaking the immediate fit between the subjective structures and the objective structures, destroys self-evidence practically. *It is when the social world loses its character as a natural phenomenon that the question of the natural, or conventional character..of social facts can be raised.*
>
> (Bourdieu 1977, 168/9, emphasis added)

In the light of this discussion we can turn our attention to the environment, and in particular the production of wastes, as a useful example of embodied behaviour. The underlying social commitments which drive our consumption, and contribute to waste, are afforded value by being naturalised. Their value is not interrogated. It is sometimes asserted that the public response to environmental issues is difficult to ascertain (Dudley 1990). However, this public response only rarely loses its character as a natural phenomenon, and is removed from scrutiny. Normally, an absence of controversy characterises the practices of a society, making them part of the dominant discourse.

If embodiment serves to ensure that environmental practices are institutionalised and unquestioned, the way that we view the relationship between the intentions of our actions, and their outcomes, is governed by *distanciation*. Distanciation refers to the way we distance ourselves in causal relationships. When actions and consequences are separated by time, or long distances, it is frequently difficult to establish the causal link between them. The effect of time-space distanciation is to confuse the relationship between intention, action, and outcome:

> social systems [become] increasingly 'stretched' across time and space, [and] the link between social activity and spatial location becomes ever more tenuous, and space itself becomes commodified and constructed.
>
> (Held and Thompson 1989, 8)

The concept of distanciation has clear utility in helping to explain the way that environmental costs are passed on to others, in space and time. For example, the Japanese car industry, operating at the global level, has sought to reduce pollution at home, by transferring car production plants to other locations. However, the existence of economic globalisation also redistributes environmental costs and benefits. Whether or not it is the intention of Japanese car producers to externalise their environmental costs can be debated. Opposition to the practice of externalisation of environmental costs is difficult to mount, because it is so often invisible, or is associated with other supposed benefits. Some of these, such as the provision of new employment opportunities in Malaysia or North East England, are only too real to those employed at a distance.

Another example is provided by the international food system. Goodman and Redclift argue that:

> with (the) simultaneous access to geographically separate production zones, the formation of the world market freed industrial capitals from the seasonality of individual national

agricultures, approximating the continuous production process
characteristic of industry.

(Goodman and Redclift 1991, 96)

In this case the technological possibilities of modern food manufacture have served to relocate the costs of the agricultural and food
production process, and in ways which are rarely linked to the
technical processes themselves. The physical environment becomes
the repository of polluted materials, and health risks increase, without
the relationship between cause and effect being clear.

The concepts of embodiment and distanciation, originating in different literatures and discourses, are nevertheless closely linked
together. Our environmental practices are routinely embodied, not
merely in our social life, but in our language and thinking. At the same
time, our actions provide a denial of the connectedness between the
origins of environmental problems and their consequences. It is not
so much that the consequences are not foreseen as that we do not
wish to see them. Many of the processes which govern our environment are established at the global level. They exist at this level not
because they are international in origin, but because they are
totalising processes, often difficult to divorce from economic activities
themselves. Global relations, in this sense, are embodied in myriad
local practices.

The material processes that govern the production of wastes, and
the capacity of natural sinks to absorb these wastes, are linked to
their ideological representations. We seldom question these representations since they are 'natural'. We need to develop a much better
understanding of the links between the way we metabolise nature,
and the values that govern this metabolism. Until we do so, we will
not be able to make workable international agreements, because we
will not be able to undo, through environmental management, what
we have done through naturalising our consumption. We first need
to decide: do we stand inside our concept of the global, or outside
it? If we place ourselves inside, if we assume responsibility for our
consumption, together with our environment, then we have a real
opportunity to remove the causes of unsustainable development. In
recovering consumption we will have bequeathed sustainable social
institutions, as well as a cleaner environment, to future generations.
In the next chapter, some of the implications of this argument are
considered. Where does responsibility for the effects of our consumption lead? How do we recover our control over consumption?

Chapter Eight
Local Environmental Action

The countries of the North bear the principal responsibility for the parlous state of the global environment. Since 1860 the industrialised countries of Europe, North America and (later) Japan, have consumed more energy, created more pollution and contributed greater carbon dioxide emissions. Wasteful energy use, and the production of goods using dirty technologies, have spread to the developing world, where environmental problems are exacerbated by highly unequal distribution of resources and rapid population increase.

The task ahead requires a transitional programme, under which the North must limit its consumption, and increase its energy efficiency, enabling the South to improve the quality of life of most of the population, without breaching the delicate environmental thresholds essential to sustainability. This requirement may seem utopian, but it is by no means impractical: what is required is concerted action, and the political will to transform metabolic processes, recovering control over consumption. If both the North and the South could match Japan's energy output per capita, which is mid-way between that of the United States and China, a major shift towards global sustainability would have been achieved without necessarily suffering a reduction in per capita welfare.

However, the challenge to recover consumption extends beyond energy alone, to profligate land used to rear animals, recovering waste materials, and the sourcing of goods in ways which do not undermine sustainable systems in the South and make little contribution to real

149

welfare in the North. Market signals, as we have seen, have failed to restrain consumption because money prices do not reflect the total costs (including the environmental costs) of production, consumption and the disposal of wastes.

In addition, the structural components of the global economic system militate against sustainable development: 'free' trade frequently means passing on the costs of market economies to the environment and to low-paid workers, undermining small-scale production systems which are resource- and energy-efficient.

This chapter examines ways of finding a route out of the impasse created by unsustainable practices and policies. Solutions will require a combination of global and local action, much of it difficult to measure. The emphasis is on what we in the North need to do, rather than on the responsibilities of those in the South. In recovering consumption we need to reduce waste and pollution, but we also need to recover our power over consumption.

In the conclusion to his path-breaking book, *Ways of Seeing*, first published a quarter century ago, John Berger examined the relationship between human wants, as defined by the advertising industry, and the self-fulfillment of the individual:

> The interminable present of meaningless working hours is 'balanced' by a dreamt future in which imaginary activity replaces the passivity of the moment. In his or her day-dreams the passive worker becomes the active consumer. The working self envies the consuming self . . . Publicity turns consumption into a substitute for democracy. The choice of what one eats (or wears or drives) takes the place of significant political choice . . . The act of acquiring has taken the place of all other actions, the sense of having obliterated all other senses.
>
> (Berger 1972, 149–153)

If the effect of the consumer society is to de-politicise, then the implications for environmental action are not difficult to distinguish. What are the main elements in an alternative vision? We need to move beyond better environmental management, and eco-efficiency, important as that is, to embrace practices which themselves enable environmental space to be used more efficiently, and ecological footprints to be clearly plotted, and their impacts reduced. This requires local action to achieve environmental goals within a context set by greater global equality.

In the case of the United Kingdom this means galvanising the energy released through the Local Agenda 21 process, under which local authorities have drawn up plans to consult with citizens, to develop best practice on local sustainability, and to support practical steps in areas such as energy management, waste reduction and disposal, and community-level employment. Examples of local action in each of these areas need to be considered before considering the wider links between local accountability and global policies. First, action is needed to help make work more sustainable.

CREATING SUSTAINABLE EMPLOYMENT: LETS SCHEMES

Local Exchange Trading Systems (LETS) schemes, have attracted attention in a number of countries in the last few years, because of their promise to combine useful employment with community interdependence. A LETS is a non-profitmaking trading system which uses an alternative local means of exchange instead of money. The principal aim is to encourage trade and exchange between participants in the scheme, rewarding people for the use of their skills and bringing benefits to those whose consumer power is limited. LETS tokens, called by a variety of different names under different schemes, are used alongside official or legal tender, by matching local needs to local resources.

LETS operates in the following way. Individuals form a LETS group, compile a directory of their various skills, services and goods, together with an inventory of their requests. A system of locally recorded accounts is kept. Each member of the LETS group starts with their account at zero. In buying goods or services through the LETS group, each member writes a cheque which is cleared with the 'bank', debiting one account and crediting the other. No money changes hands in this system. Just as a cheque simply records information in a normal bank account so, under the LETS system, there is a record kept of each transaction. However, unlike a commercial bank account, LETS balances are open to public scrutiny.

The LETS system functions like barter, enabling trade to take place without the use of money. LETS also overcomes the disadvantages of barter, however, by providing a means of exchange which provides asymmetrical, rather than simply bilateral, trading. As the primary objective is to facilitate the exchange of goods and services, rather than the pursuit of profit, there is no interest charged, or accruing, to individual accounts. Perhaps the single greatest benefit of LETS is that it helps to reinforce ties between people, by enabling individuals to go into debit. Indeed the system encourages them to do so, since this prompts them to offer services to others.

In the view of some commentators, the success of LETS schemes in North America proves that it is an economic expression of grass-roots, community-based action, appropriate for developed, industrial societies (Greco 1994, Linton and Greco 1994). The emphasis is local in scale, and geared to local markets and employment. It is also claimed that LETS reinforces the ties between people, rather than forcing them into competition with each other on the labour market. It encourages diversification, and helps preserve traditional skills. At the same time LETS schemes are democratic and accountable, free from hierarchy and the dimensions of power that permeate the formal market economy. LETS schemes encourage local self-reliance, and the de-coupling of the local economy from the national, or international one. Indeed, some have argued that LETS schemes are, in effect, a form of social learning, providing members with both a practice, and a vision, of an alternative society (Greco 1994).

Today there are approximately 250 LETS schemes in the UK compared with only half a dozen or so in 1991. Estimates suggest that about ten thousand people are engaged in LETS schemes in over two hundred localities, in the UK (LETSlink 1994).

It has been suggested that LETS enables the individual to make a link between their identity as citizens, and that of consumers (and producers), at the same time facilitating their organisational powers at the local level. The notion of altruism, which many believe is a feature of much environmental action, is translated through LETS into a convergence between community- and self-interest. Everybody benefits from inclusion in LETS networks, and they enable individuals to recover some control, democratically exercised, over the use to which their own labour and skills are put. At the same time the power of the consumer to buy goods is harnessed to local needs, and those of fellow citizens.

Research that is currently underway explores the roots of LETS, and compares LETS activities with those of other ecological groups (Barry and Proops 1995). It also explores what is sustainable within LETS, a definition of value which makes a virtue of indebtedness and a vice of 'accumulation'. LETS is also significant in affording weight to the quality of life, rather than to quantitative measures. Unlike some indices for measuring sustainable development, for example, LETS provides an alternative to mainstream economic activity, rather than assessing growth in a different way.

At the same time, critics of LETS argue that it is largely successful as a complement to the orthodox market, rather than a substitute for it, and is incapable of wider consolidation, in time or space. It is too early to say whether LETS schemes are the precursor of something very radical – a move towards the 'steady-state' economy – or merely an adjustment to an enduring capitalist system, made possible by high rates of under-employment.

BEYOND RECYCLING: RECOVERING OUR CONTROL OVER WASTE

Citizens of the industrialised countries, and large numbers of people in the South, are increasingly faced by growing problems in managing and disposing of wastes. These are partly the legacy of unsustainable practices in the past, and partly a result of environmental management itself, for finding technical solutions to problems may actually exacerbate their causes.

For almost half a century there have been demands for accurate information on the extent of contaminated land in the United Kingdom (Watson 1993). Not until 1985, when the Royal Commission on Environmental Pollution interested itself in the matter, was there anything approaching a public debate. The Commission acknowledged that local authorities and communities faced difficulties in developing land that was already contaminated, but also 'insisted that available technical solutions could "solve" most cases of contamination'. The main problem, in the words of the Commission, was:

> to ensure a systematic approach to the provision of adequate information and advice for local authorities to identify contaminated sites at an early stage in the planning process ...

> (Watson 1993, 174)

The long-drawn-out process to compile registers of contaminated sites met the opposition of virtually every professional group interested in land redevelopment: chartered surveyors, land-fill operators, and many local authorities. Even the commercial banks opposed the keeping of registers, in the belief that they might have to meet the clean-up costs.

In July 1992 an official way around the problem seemed to have been found: to declassify most sites as contaminated. The number of contaminated uses was cut down from 50 to 8, excluding tanneries, docks, paint manufacturers, munitions manufacture and testing, sewage works and electrical equipment disposal. The Royal Commission on Environmental Pollution publicly condemned the draft document, claiming that:

> it is hard to avoid the conclusion that this marked reduction in the scope of the registers will make protecting the environment, and carrying out remedial work, even more difficult.
>
> (Royal Commission on Environmental Pollution 1992)

Official figures for contaminated land in Britain suffer from a number of shortcomings. First, they do not include sites in active use, most land-fill sites, and very small sites. In addition, official figures only deal with direct contamination, they do not include wastes that have been dispersed over a large area. Thus, while the Department of the Environment refers to a maximum of 27,000 hectares, other serious estimates put the figure much higher, possibly as much as 75,000 sites affecting over 100,000 hectares (*ENDS* 1991). The opposition of local people to contaminated sites rarely makes headline news in the national press, but it has occurred, and is occurring, wherever the public is aware of the cloak of secrecy shrouding the facts. Information about 'closed sites', of which six thousand exist in the United Kingdom, cannot officially be divulged.

Friends of the Earth, and other campaigning groups, have sought to illuminate the problem, producing guides to affected sites, and linking up with local campaigns. In the meantime the most common 'management' strategies involve on-site containment, covering contaminated land with earth or tarmac, while cheap waste disposal in land-fills is undermining the relatively modest programmes for treating solid wastes.

The underlying problem is not addressed and, together with secrecy and official indecision, serves to compound the problem. Technical solutions are proposed to what are essentially social choices. There has been enormous official encouragement for incineration of waste, as an alternative to land-fill. Incineration reduces the volume of material going to land-fill. It concentrates the toxics into a dense powdery ash, which is less dangerous than most domestic rubbish, and easier to move. Incineration also destroys most of the organic material which can cause methane generation in landfill sites, as well as polluting the air and encouraging vermin. In addition, most modern incinerators yield some energy, which can be offset against operating costs and, although incinerators produce polluted air, state-of-the-art pollution control equipment can reduce this substantially (Connett 1994).

There are also considerable disadvantages to incineration as a means of waste disposal. The gains in land-fill space are of the order of two or three times those of conventional methods – much less than the tenfold benefits sometimes claimed. Similarly it is clear that better methods of air pollution control, which reduce the amount of toxins going into the atmosphere, also contribute to more toxicity in the ash which remains after incineration (Connett 1994). The disposal of toxic ash can present new challenges to waste management, that many local authorities are in a poor position to meet. Incinerators do not solve environmental problems; they create new ones, and in the process help promote more official secrecy and less official disclosure. Incinerators are expensive to install and run, yet show a poor economic return for the investment. They create little employment and transfer funds from local authorities to multinational engineering and consulting companies.

The main advantage of waste incineration as a disposal strategy is one that is rarely mentioned. This is that incineration does not require changes in the consumer's behaviour, and local authorities do not have to reorganise the community infrastructure involving house-holds, industrial plant and waste-handlers. There is no need, at either the local or national level, to draw attention to the underlying social commitments which drive the production of waste.

Like many other elements of the 'engineered solution', modern state-of-the-art waste incinerators provide a technically sophisticated answer to the wrong question. As Paul and Ellen Connett put it, 'the problem is not how to perfect the destruction of discarded resources, but how to recover them' (Connett 1994, 19). The solution lies, as many local activists have shown, with reducing the volume of waste, initiating recycling programmes and expanding composting.

Most environmental management is reactive, responding to pollution only when problems become very severe, or human health is involved. This reactive approach makes use of indicators on the pressure-state-response (PSR) model, as used by the Organisation for Economic Cooperation and Development (OECD) and the national governments of the Netherlands, Norway and Canada. For example, the pressure of acid rain leads to increased acidification of the environment and we respond, by putting catalytic converters on cars. These kinds of end-of-pipe measures are necessary, but not sufficient.

There are several problems in this approach. The impacts of pollutants on the environment tend to be more complex than the models we use to understand them. They also change over time, bringing unanticipated effects. Many impacts do not become apparent for long periods of time. Policy responses, such as water treatment and waste incineration, then prove inappropriate in the face of a new round of environmental effects, such as the increase in sludge and the emission of carcinogenic dioxides. End-of-pipe 'solutions', then, tend to be not only environmentally out-dated very quickly, but also extremely costly.

Radical solutions to the management of waste will require very difficult political solutions. Particularly in cities, the generation of waste can reach continental proportions, since urban centres funnel resources from rural areas, and transform them at the point of sale, multiplying problems of disposal many times over. The city of New York is a case in point (Outerbridge 1994). It has been suggested that of the massive quantities of organic waste produced every day in New York City, a significant amount could be safely and economically composted. Pilot schemes have shown that composting is technically feasible, although there are difficulties in sorting, collecting and transporting waste. The solutions to waste management on the scale of large cities are therefore necessarily bound up with the solutions to even larger and inter-connected environmental problems: the inter-urban transport system, the location of supermarkets, even the components of the agri-food system at the global level.

FARMERS' NETWORKS

Even the problems of the agri-food system at the global level can be addressed, to a limited degree, by local action. During the last decade the Fairtrade movement has grown in strength in many of the developed countries (Vidal 1996). Within the context of a global trading system that places little emphasis on social justice or environmental sustainability, 'fair trade' represents a small but vital attempt to address the global problem. In Nicaragua, for example, small-scale coffee producers are offered a guaranteed minimum price for their product which is significantly higher than that of the New York coffee exchange. They are provided with realistic credit, advice and – most importantly – a guaranteed market for their produce. The producers, in return, agree to meet reasonable environmental standards. The coffee buyers pay for the right to use the seal of approval, or Fairtrade marque, administered in the United Kingdom by the Fairtrade Foundation, and in Europe by the Max Havelaar Foundation.

The effect of these arrangements on the price of each cup of coffee is small – it costs perhaps one penny a cup extra through the Fairtrade network. As in many other poor, coffee-producing countries, buyers in Nicaragua are often unscrupulous, and markets function along arbitrary lines. The middlemen – or *coyotes* – take advantage of the peasant farmers' ignorance of markets, and inability to influence them. At the same time, the middlemen themselves are vulnerable to the big multi-national trading companies who ship most of the coffee to Europe and North America. Finally, as with other commodity markets, there is an additional level of speculators, whose interest is simply in gaining short-term advantages from unpredictable trade and harvests.

Today, in the developed world, Fairtrade is growing apace. For almost a decade, sales of fairly traded coffee have increased in Europe by almost six per cent a year, even in the face of declining sales during the recession. As quoted by John Vidal in *The Guardian*, one of the founders of Fairtrade, Brian Chapman, expresses confidence that people everywhere want to trade more fairly, enjoy quality products and, importantly, protect the environment. This is particularly true of many younger people, who represent a growing share of the market (Vidal 1996). In fact relatively few people are aware of the social and environmental costs of producing commodities like coffee in a way that is environmentally sustainable and socially just. Campaigns to draw the attention of the public to fair trade represent an important element in the movement to combat waste and exploitation at the global level, and provide material evidence of what local action can produce.

Some campaigns have targeted the producer as well as the consumer. A good example is the network of farmers known as 'The Farmers' World Network' which aims to link farmers in the United Kingdom with other farmers in Europe and beyond. The 'Farmers' Third World Network', as it was then called, was formed during the famine in Ethiopia in 1984. At the time, many farmers were involved in the campaign to 'send a tonne' to the victims of famine in Africa.

This prompted some British farmers to question the long-term objectives of voluntary famine-relief. Aidan Harrison, a North-umberland farmer, wrote an article for *Farmers Weekly*, calling for more than aid to be given to Ethiopia. He argued that people were going hungry in many parts of the world, while food surpluses were being built up in Europe. He wondered whether the inequalities of the trading system could be addressed, so that food could get where it was needed. He went on to propose that a network of farmers should be formed, to exchange ideas and to try and find ways of alleviating the root causes of famine. This network would begin with farmers themselves, and examine the agricultural systems employed by farmers in the developed world. In addition it was proposed to offer expertise to farmers from the 'Third World' if this was appropriate and, in addition, seek to influence international farm policy through political lobbying.

The Farmers' World Network has developed during the last decade, providing a forum for farmers to meet, exchange information, and contribute to the debate about sustainable farming systems. The movement has spread to agricultural colleges in the United Kingdom and, as their journal *Food Matters Worldwide* illustrates, the issues have broadened to include not only farming practices, but food consumption, and the aid and trade policies which disadvantage poor farmers, especially in the South.

In his original paper, Harrison drew on the experience of another organisation working with farmers, centred in France. The French farmers' network had come into being to bypass the vast schemes for introducing high-technology agriculture in the developing world. Many farmers in France were suspicious of the benefits of such schemes, and critical of their government's involvement. Many of these French farmers later went on to make changes in their own farming practices, such as refusing to use imported feed from Latin America, which they believed would free farmers in the South to concentrate on their own communities' needs. Consumption would be returned to local people. Aidan Harrison also emphasised the need for British farmers to inform themselves of the issues behind agricultural trade, and to lobby on behalf of fair trade.

In the aftermath of the debate initiated by Harrison, the Farmers' World Network came into being, a successful application for funding was made to the European Union, and a regular cycle of activities took place. These were jointly organised by Voluntary Service Overseas (VSO) which was targeting agricultural colleges, and launching a development education project of its own. The links between farmers have assumed importance, since it was the realisation that British farmers might influence the occurence of poverty in the developing countries which prompted the start of the movement. It dawned on some farmers that there were lessons to be learned from the developing countries, as well as advice to proffer. One British farmer, writing in *Food Matters Worldwide* expresses the force of this connection in the following way:

> I used to grow maize on one of my hillside fields, which was a nice dry field and useful as a dung-spreading area during the winter. It was only after half a winter of hauling dung out to the field that I really considered that it might be prone to erosion, as there were no weeds on it and nothing to hold the topsoil in place. Yet when I was at agricultural college learning the techniques of growing maize nobody ever stressed that any field being prepared for the crop would be a bare slope in mid-winter. I learned all about growing maize and very little about soil erosion. Yet the subject is the chief topic of conversation among farmers all over the Third World. I now grow my maize on about the only flat field on the farm!

> (Nick Viney quoted in *Farmers' World Network* 1991)

These examples of campaigns and activities in the North point to the interconnectedness of issues: consumption is linked to income and employment, but also to the volume and quality of waste. Food and other commodities have environmental impacts both at home and abroad. Local campaigns are often particularly well-placed to draw attention to these interconnections, and to combine political lobbying with practical action by individuals – as consumers, citizens and producers.

Searching for practical solutions to some of the problems analysed in this book forces us to re-examine our own part in these problems. This is frequently an uncomfortable experience. The goal of much conventional waste management today, as documented in the 1995 White Paper (DOE 1995), is the increased capacity to absorb waste – it is at the 'disposal' end of the 'waste hierachy' (reduction/re-use/recovery/disposal). However, the principal challenge, as argued in this book, is to reduce the flow of materials and energy through the economy (the metabolic throughput) by gearing our production, and consumption, to the capacities of nature, of natural sinks and resource systems.

Recovering our power over consumption rests with restructuring trade relations, replacing so-called 'free trade' with fairer trade, and assuming new global priorities in the process. At the end of the twentieth century, consumption is worshipped, almost as an alternative to democracy. However, without the democratic involvement of people, and more democratically accountable institutions, the environment will continue to attract almost as much rhetoric as it does waste. As the distinguished Norwegian anthropologist, Fredrik Barth, has observed:

> Something far more fundamental is needed: new institutions that will facilitate rational individual and collective decisions in a full world condition, and a human morality that can guide such decisions in such a way as to secure a future for life on earth.

> (Barth 1996)

References

Agarwal, A and Narain, S (1991) *Global Warming in an Unequal World*, Centre for Science and Environment, New Delhi.

Allmark, T (1994) Entropy and Sinks, M.Sc. dissertation, Rural Resources and Environmental Policy, Wye College, University of London.

Ayres, RU and Simonis, UE (eds) (1994) *Industrial Metabolism*, United Nations University Press, Tokyo.

Ayres, RU (1994) 'Industrial metabolism: Theory and Policy' in Ayres and Simonis (eds).

Barry, J and Proops, J (1995) 'Local Employment and Trade Systems: linking citizenship and sustainability', University of Keele Economics Department.

Barth, F (1996) 'Global cultural diversity in a "full world economy"' in Arizpe, L (ed) *The Cultural Dimensions of Global Change*, UNESCO, Paris.

Baudrillard, J (1981) *For a Critique of the Political Economy of the Sign*, Telos Press, St Louis.

Berger, J (1972) *Ways of Seeing*, Harmondsworth, Penguin.

Bertram, G (1992) 'Tradeable emission permits and the control of greenhouse gases' *The Journal of Development Studies* 28 (423–446).

Bhaskar, V and Glyn, A (eds) (1995) *The North, the South and the Environment*, Earthscan/United Nations University Press, London.

Bird, J, Curtis, B, Putnam, T, Robertson, G and Tickner, L (1993) *Mapping the Futures*, Routledge

Bourdieu, P (1977) *Outline of a Theory of Practice*, Cambridge University Press, Cambridge.

161

Bramwell, A (1989) *Ecology in the Twentieth Century*, Yale University Press.

Brandt Commission Report (1980) *North–South: A Programme for Survival*, Pan Books, London.

Brewer, J and Porter, R (1993) *Consumption and the World of Goods*, Routledge, London.

Briggs, Asa (1988) *Victorian Things*, Batsford, London.

Brimblecombe, P (1990) 'Writing on Smoke' in Bradby, H (ed) *Dirty Words*, Earthscan, London.

Brown, K and Adger, N (1993) 'A UK greenhouse gas inventory: on estimating anthropogenic and natural sources and sinks', *Ambio* 22 (509–517).

Brown, K, Jordan, A and Turner, K (1993) 'Global environmental change and mechanisms for North–South resource transfers', *Journal of International Development* 5 (571–589).

Brundtland Commission (WCED) (1987) *Our Common Future*, Oxford University Press, Oxford.

Cadman, JD (1989) 'Energy from the Amazon', *Civil Engineering* December (54–57).

Cadman, JD (1993) 'Energy and environment in the Brazilian Amazon region', *Pedasa*, Brasilia.

Cairncross, F (1991) *Costing the Earth*, Economist Books, London.

Campbell, C (1991) 'The sociology of consumption' in D Miller, (ed) *Acknowledging Consumption*, Routledge, London.

Catton, W and Dunlap, R (1994) 'Struggling with human exemptionalism' *The American Sociologist* 25, Spring.

Chatterjee, P and Finger, M (1994) *The Earth Brokers*, Routledge, London.

China Daily (1993) February 17.

Clapp, J (1994) 'Dumping On The Poor', Global Security Programme, Occasional Paper no. 5, University of Cambridge, August.

Commission of the European Communities (1993) *Growth, Competitiveness and Employment*, White Paper, Office for Official Publications of the European Communities, Luxembourg.

Connett, E (1994) 'Municipal waste incineration: wrong question, wrong answer', *The Ecologist* 24(1).

Daly, H (1992) *Steady-State Economics*, second edition, Earthscan, London.

Delbeke, A (1991) 'European policies for environmental protection', in T Barker (ed) *Green Futures for Economic Growth*, Cambridge Econometrics, Cambridge.

Department of the Environment (DOE) (1995) *Making Waste Work: a strategy for sustainable waste management in England and Wales*, HMSO, London.

Department of the Environment (DOE) (1993) *Climate Change*, United Kingdom National Programme for Carbon Dioxide Emissions, DOE, London.

Di Lascio, M and Di Lascio, V (1993) 'Calculating Brazil's energy needs', *Pedasa*, Brasilia.

Dudley, N (1990) 'Changing public perceptions of air pollution' in Bradby, H (ed) *Dirty Words*, Earthscan, London.

Dunlop, RE (1993) 'From Environmental to Ecological Problems', in Calhounad, C and Ritzer, G (eds) *Social Problems*, McGraw-Hill, New York.

Durning, AT (1992) *How Much Is Enough?* Earthscan, London.

The Economist (1993) December 11, Economist Newspapers.

The Economist (1994a) 'The global economy', October 1, Economist Newspapers.

The Economist (1994b) 'Holes galore', October 15, Economist Newspapers.

Eden, M (1988) 'Colonos, agriculture and adaptation in the Colombian Amazon', *Journal of Biogeography* 15 (79–85).

Eden, M (1990) *Ecology and Land Management in Amazonia*, Belhaven Press, London.

Ekins, P (1993) 'Trading Off The Future', The New Economics Foundation, London.

ENDS (1991) '£10–£30 billion and still rising – UK contaminated food clean up', *ENDS Bulletin* 201, October/January.

Ewell, PT and Poleman, TT (1980) *Uxpanapa: Agricultural Development in the Mexican Tropics*, Pergamon, Oxford.

Farmers' World Network (1991) *Food Matters Worldwide* 12, July (21–29).

Featherstone, M (1990) (ed), *Global Culture*, Sage, London.

Filho, AV (1993) 'O Plano 2015 da Electrobras e a amazonia', *Pedasa*, Brasilia.

Fischer-Kowalski, M and Haberl, H (1994) 'The Cultural Evolution of Social Metabolism with Nature', XIII World Congress of Sociology, Bielefeld, ms.

Fleming, D (1994) 'Towards the low-output economy: the future that the Delors White Paper tries not to face', *European Environment*, July.

Friends of the Earth (1992) *Response to the United Kingdom Government's Submission to the Commission for Sustainable Development*, FOE, London.

Gadgil, M and Guha, R (1995) *Ecology and Equity*, Routledge, London.

Gleick, J (1987) *Chaos: Making a New Science*, Heinemann, London.

Global 2000 (1982) *Report to the President*, Harmondsworth, Penguin.

Goodland, R (1995) 'The concept of environmental sustainability', *Annual Review of Ecological Systems* 26, 1–24.

Goodland, R and Daly, H (1992) 'An Ecological–Economic Assessment of Deregulation of International Commerce Under GATT', Environment Department, World Bank, Washington DC.

Goodland, R, Daly, H and Serafy, H (1992) *Population, Technology, Lifestyle*, Island Press, New York.

Goodman, DE and Redclift, MR (1991) *Refashioning Nature: Food, Ecology, Culture*, Routledge, London.

Goudie, A (1986) *The Human Impact on the Natural Environment*, Blackwell, Oxford.

Greco, TH (1994) *New Money for Healthy Communities*, Greco Publishing, Tucson, Arizona.

Grove, R and Anderson, D (1987) *Conservation in Africa*, Cambridge University Press, Cambridge.

Grubb, M (1991) *Energy Policies and the Greenhouse Effect* volume one, RIIA/Dartmouth Publishing Company, Aldershot.

Grubb, M, Koch, M, Munson, A, Sullivan, F and Thomson, K (1993) *The Earth Summit Agreement*, Earthscan, London.

Habermas, J (1971) *Theory and Practice*, Heinemann, London.

Hall, C (1985) 'Working at the World Bank' in T Hayter and C Watson (eds) *Aid, Rhetoric and Reality*, Pluto Press, London.

Held, D and Thompson, J (eds) (1989) *Social Theory of Modern Society: Giddens and his Critics*, Cambridge University Press, Cambridge.

HMSO (1994) *Social Trends 1990/91*, HMSO, London.

Holmberg, J, Bass, S and Timberlake, L (1991) *Defending the Future*, Earthscan, London.

Huber, J (1982) *Die verlorene Unschuld der Okologie*, Fisher, Frankfurt.

Humphrey, CR and Buttel, F (1982) *Environment, Energy and Society*, Wadsworth, Belmont, California.

IBRD (International Bank for Reconstruction and Development) (1989) *World Development Report*, Washington DC.

IBRD (1990) *Energy Demand in the Developing Countries: prospects for the future*, IBRD Commodity Working Paper no. 23, Washington DC.

IBRD (1992) *World Development Report*, Washington DC.

IDB (Interamerican Development Bank) (1991) *Amazonia Without Myths*, Commission on Development and Environment for Amazonia, IDB/UNDP, Washington DC.

IIED (International Institute for Environment and Development) (1992) 'Rio: the lessons learned', *Perspectives* 9, issue title.

Illich, I (1975) *Tools For Conviviality*, Fontana, London.

Jacobs, M (1991) *The Green Economy*, Pluto Press, London.

Jordan, A (1993) 'The International Organisational Machinery for Sustainable Development: Rio and the Road Beyond', CSERGE Working Paper GEC 93–11, CSERGE, London.

Jordan, A (1994) 'Financing the UNCED Agenda: the vexed question of additionality', *Environment* March (16–27).

Krause, F, Bach, W and Kooney, J (1990) *Energy Policy in the Greenhouse*, Earthscan, London.

Lash, S (1990) *Sociology of Postmodernism*, Routledge, London.

Lee, M (1993) *Consumer Culture Reborn*, Routledge, London.

LETSlink (1994) *The LETSinfo Pack*, LETS Development Agency, Warminster, United Kingdom.

Liberatore, A (1993) 'Beyond The Earth Summit', European University Working Paper 93/5, Florence.

Liberatore, A (1994) 'Facing global warming: the interactions between science and policymaking in the European Community', in M Redclift and T Benton (eds) *Social Theory and the Global Environment*, Routledge, London.

Linton, M and Greco, TH (1994) 'The Local Employment and Trading System', *Whole Earth Review* 55.

Long, Helen (1993) *The Edwardian House*, Manchester University Press, Manchester.

Lovelock, J (1995) 'The greening of science', in Tom Wakeford and Martin Walters (eds) *Science for the Earth*, Wiley, London.

Marshall, T (1994) 'Dimensions of Sustainable Development', Paper presented to the conference on the Politics of Sustainable Development, Rethimnon, Crete.

Maslow, A (1954) *Motivation and Personality*, Harper and Row, New York.

Mauss, M (1954) *The Gift*, Cohen and West, London.

Max-Neef, M (1991) 'Development and human needs' in P Ekins and M Max-Neef (eds) *Real-Life Economics*, Routledge, London.

McGowan, F (1992) 'Moveable Objects and Resistible Forces: the European Electricity Industry and EC Regulatory Reform', SPRU, Sussex University.

Meadows, DM, Meadows, DL, Randers, J and Behrens, WW (1972) *Limits To Growth*, Pan Books, London.

Meadows, DH, Meadows, D and Randers, DH (1992) *Beyond the Limits to Growth*, Earthscan.

Miller, D (1987) *Material Culture and Mass Consumption*, Blackwell, Oxford.

Miller, D (1994) (ed) *Acknowledging Consumption*, Routledge, London.

Molion, LC (1993) 'Vegetal Diesel: the renewable energy source', *Pedasa*, Brasilia.

Moreira, JR (1993) 'Biomass and electric power', *Pedasa*, Brasilia.

Morris, C (1991) 'Introduction', in *Selections from William Cobbett's Rural Rides, 1821–1832*, Webb and Bower.

Mougeot, L (1985) 'River impoundment, related population displacement in Brazilian Amazonia: the Tucurui resettlement program (TRP) 1976–1984', International Congress of Americanists Congress, Bogota.

Nairobi Declaration on Climate Change (1990) African Centre for Technology Centre, Nairobi.

New Economics Foundation (1994) *Sustainability Indicators*, NEF, London.

Norgaard, R (1981) 'Sociosystem and ecosystem co-evolution in the Amazon', *Journal of Environmental Economics and Management* 8 (238–254).

Norgaard, R (1993) *Development Betrayed*, Routledge, London.

OECD (Organisation for Economic Cooperation and Development) (1991) *The State of the Environment*, Paris.

O'Keefe, P, Middleton, N and Moao, S (1993) *Tears of the Crocodile*, Pluto Press, London.

(OST) Office of Science and Technology (1993) *Realising Our Potential*, HMSO, London.

Outerbridge, T (1994) 'The big backyard: composting strategies in New York City', *The Ecologist* 24(3) May/June.

Pahl, R and Wallace, C (1985) 'Household work strategies in economic recession' in Nanneke Redclift and Enzo Mingione (eds), *Beyond Employment*, Blackwell, Oxford.

Parikh, J (1991) *Consumption Patterns: the driving force of environmental stress*, Indira Gandhi Institute of Research, Bombay.

Parnwell, M and Bryant, R (1996) (eds) *Environmental Change in South-East Asia: People, Politics and Sustainable Development*, Routledge, London.

Pearce, D (1991) (ed) *Blueprint Two*, Earthscan, London.

Pearce, D, Markandya, A and Barbier, E (1989) *Blueprint for a Green Economy*, Earthscan, London.

Pearson, P (1995) 'Environmental priorities in different development, situations: electricity, environment and development', in Y Guerrier, N Alexander, J Chase and M O'Brien, (eds) *Values and the Environment*, Wiley, Chichester.

Pedasa (1993) 'Propostas Para Uma Politica Energetica Para O Desenvolvimento Auto-Sustentado Na Amazonia: Resultantes Do Pedasa '93', (Pedasa) Document presented to the President of Brazil, November 11, 1993, Brasilia.

Porritt, J (1984) *Seeing Green*, Blackwell, Oxford.

Raghavan, C (1993) 'GEF Meet Ends in Disagreement', *Third World Resurgence* 41 (17–29).

RCEP (Royal Commission on Environmental Pollution) (1992) 'Contaminated Land in the United Kingdom', London.

Redclift, M (1993a) 'The Structural Origins of Environmental Problems: lessons from Mexico?', Paper presented to the Research Workshop on Agriculture, Poverty and the Environment after Structural Adjustment, Bangalore, India, 10–12 October.

Redclift, M (1995) 'The environment and structural adjustment: lessons for policy interventions in the 1990s', *Journal of Environmental Management* 44 (55–68).

Redclift, M and Woodgate, G (1993b) *Concepts of the Environment in the Social Sciences*, External Programme, Wye College, University of London.

Reed, D (1992) *Structural Adjustment and the Environment*, Westview Press, Boulder, Colorado.

Rothwell, R (1992) 'Industrial innovation and government environmental regulation: some lessons from the past' *Technovation* 12(7) (447–458).

Royal Commission on Environmental Pollution (1992), letter to the Department of the Environment, 2 October.

Sachs, W (1991) 'Environment and development: the story of a dangerous liaison', *The Ecologist* 21(6), November/December.

Schor, J (1995) 'Can the North stop consumption growth? Escaping the cycle of work and spend', in Bhaskar, V and Glyn, A (eds), *The North, the South and the Environment*, Earthscan, London.

Schumacher, EF (1973) *Small is Beautiful*, Harper and Row, New York.

Smith, JH, Alvim, P, Homma, A, Falesi, I and Serrao, A (1991) 'Environmental impacts of resource exploitation in Amazonia', *Global Environmental Change* 4, September (313–320).

Thompson, M (1990) 'The management of hazardous wastes and the hazards of wasteful management', in Bradby, H (ed) *Dirty Words*, Earthscan, London.

Tolba, MK, Osama, A, El-Kholy, OA (1992) (eds), *The World Environment 1972–1992*, Chapman and Hall, London.

UNED (United Nations Environment and Development) UK Committee (1995) *Sustaining Development since the Rio Summit*, UNED-UK, London.

UNEP (United Nations Environment Programme) (1991) *Environmental Data Report*, Nairobi, Kenya.

UNEP (United Nations Environment Programme) (1994) *World Resources: a guide to the global environment*, Oxford University Press, Oxford.

United Kingdom Environmental Foresight Project (1993), HMSO, London.

Urry, J (1995) *Consuming Places*, Routledge.

Veblen, T (1899) *The Theory of the Leisure Class*, Macmillan, New York.

Vidal, J (1996) 'Hope sprouts in the beanfields', *The Guardian*, March 6.

Ward, B (1979) *Progress For A Small Planet*, Penguin, Harmondsworth.

Watson, A (1993) 'Britain's Toxic Legacy' *The Ecologist*, vol 23, no 5, September/October.

WCED (World Commission on Environment and Development) (1987) *Our Common Future*, Oxford University Press, Oxford.

Wells, P and Jetter, M (1991) *The Global Consumer*, Victor Gollanz.

World Conservation Strategy (WCS) (1983) International Union for the Conservation of Nature (IUCN), Gland, Switzerland.

World Conservation Strategy (WCS) (1991) *Caring for the Earth*, International Union for the Conservation of Nature, Gland, Switzerland.

World Resources Institute (WRI) (1991) *Greenhouse Warming: Negotiating a Global Regime*, Washington DC.

Wynne, B (1994) 'Scientific knowledge and the global environment', in M Redclift and T Benton (eds), *Social Theory and the Global Environment*, Routledge, London.

Zylberstajn, D and Souza, NM (1993) 'The aluminium industry energy consumption in Northern Brazil: facts and trends', *Pedasa*, Brasilia.

Index

'Additionality' 21, 26, 29

Agenda 21 11, 28–29, 32, 37, 54, 151; *see also* United Nations Conference on Environment and Development (UNCED)

Agriculture 113, 156–160

Air pollution 61, 86, 140, 144, 155; *see also* Emissions, Greenhouse gases

Amazon: energy policies 100–108

Asia: pollution 86

Auditing: environmental 114–115

Behaviour: environmental impacts of 2, 138–141, 150; *see also* Sociology

Berger, John 150

Biodiversity: and UNCED 21, 27–28

Bourdieu, Pierre 145

Brandt Report 14

Brazil: energy consumption 9 energy production 102–108; energy policy 91–92, 100–108; and population 101, 107

Bretton Woods institutions 12, 35

Brimblecombe: and language 144–145

Carbon budgets 126–128, 143

Cars: and classes 121; and pollution 38, 49, 83–86, 116, 140, 147, 155–156

CFCs 44, 81, 93, 116

China: future consumption 76–79 pollution 86

Climate change: and UNCED 21, 23–26; extent of 35–36; and Global Circulation Models (GCMs) 35–36

Consumption: and anthropology 5; and behaviour 138–141; and development 3–4; classes 119–123; costs of 114–117; energy 62–72, 79–82; and environment 5–8; *see also* Recovering consumption

Contaminated land 153–154

Commission on Sustainable Development 54,117

Critical loads 114–115

Culture: and attitudes 140; and consumption 4, 145; *see also* Lifestyle and Sociology

Daly, Herman: and 'steady-state' economics 2; and sustainability 4

Democracy: and environment 117–119

Developing countries: and 'additionality' 29; and debt 32, 72; and climate change 23–26; and ecological footprints 142; emissions 25; and energy consumption 61–79; environment and development 13, 36–38, 93, 99–100, 123–129; and fairtrade 156–157; future energy consumption 76–81; future economic growth 74–81; and Global Environment Facility (GEF) 29–30, 34; and international economy 72–79, 141; poverty 72; resource consumption 121–123

Development: and Brazil 101; and consumption 3–4, 128; and development models 9, 13, 141; and ecological footprints 142; and UNCED 19–38; and the industrial revolution 41–42, 45; and politics of 118–119

Discourse: on environment 136–141, 144–148

'Distanciation' 144–148

Earth Summit *see* United Nations Conference on Environment and Development

Ecological footprints 142, 150

Economy: global 15; Mexican 14–15

Ecosystem: global 111–113

Electricity: and European production 94–96, 99, 122; *see also* Energy

'Embodiment' 144–148

Emissions: and climate change 24–25; 'livelihood' 124; measurement 54; and policy 92, 97, 99, 111; of waste 21, 44, 83, 156; *see also* Greenhouse gases

Employment: and economic growth 51; and Local Exchange Trading Schemes (LETS) 151–153

Energy: and Brazil 91–92, 100–108; and environmental impacts 80–81; and global consumption 9, 62–81, 122–123; and lifestyle 67–68; natural 45–46; and policies 91–108; and regulation 98–100; *see also* Coal, Electricity, Fossil fuels, Hydrocarbons, Nuclear power

Environmental auditing 114–115

Environmental discourse 136–141

Environmental economics 18–19, 24–25, 48, 98–99, 115–116

Environmental 'foresight' 4

Environmental quality: measurement 114–117

Europe: energy policy 91–100

European Union: and energy policy 91–100; role in sustainability 33–34, 51–52; and trade 73, 158

Evolution: and environmental change 8, 43–47

Fairtrade 156–160

Farmers' networks 156–160

Forests: Amazon 106–108; Forest principles – Earth Summit 26–27

Fourth European Community Environmental Action Programme 97

Fossil fuels 41, 47; *see also* Energy

Gaia 43, 113

Global 2000 report 15

Global Circulation Models (GCMs) 35–36

Global economy: and international policy 15–19

Global ecosystem 111–113

Global Environment Facility (GEF) 23, 26, 28–31, 34; and 'additionality' 26, 29

Global environmental change 40–47; and Earth Summit 22; and industrial revolution 41–42; and thermodynamics 42–43

Greenhouse gases: climate change 24–25, emissions 80, 81, 93, 105, 107, 122, 128–131, 143, 149; measurement 54; targets 39; *see also* Carbon budgets

'Harmonisation' 97–98

Hazardous waste: export 22, 86–89; production 68, 82; *see also* Toxic waste

History: and consumption 5

Household waste 82, 129

Hydrocarbons: and Amazon 102–103; and industrialisation 61–71, 88–90, 129

Hydropower: and Amazon 100–102, 104–108

Incinerators 154–156
Indicators: and sustainability 9, 49–59, 116–117
Industrial revolution: and global environmental change 41–42, 45
Industrialisation: and energy consumption 62–79; and environment 61, 68–71
Industrial systems 111–113, 131
Industrial waste 82
Inequality: and consumption 119–123; and economic growth 72–79, 149; and incomes 72–74; and trade 156–158; *see also* Welfare
Intellectual property rights 142–143
Intergovernmental Panel on Climate Change (IPCC) 35–36, 130
International economy 15, 72–79, 91, 141, 143–144; and inequality 72–73; and fairtrade 156–160; and future growth 74–79
International finance: and Earth Summit 28–29
International Institute for Environment and Development (IIED) 14
International environmental policy 11–38; and Brandt Report 14; and European Union 33–34; and global economy 15–19; and 'limits to growth' 13; and Montreal Protocol 30; and Stockholm conference 12–13; and World Conservation Strategies 14, 112–113, 117

Knowledge: environmental 139; and objectivism 145–146; and phenomenology 145–146; and uncertainty 136–137, 140, 144

Landfill 82–83, 113, 129, 153
Language: and environmental discourse 144–148
Lifecycle analysis 115
Lifestyle: and consumption 5–6, 8; and energy consumption 67–68; and waste 159–160; *see also* Sociology
'Limits to growth' 13, 113

Local environmental action 10, 32–33, 150–160; and farmers' networks 156–160; and Local Exchange Trading Systems (LETS) 151–153; *see also* Participation
Local Exchange Trading Systems (LETS) 151–153
Lovelock: Gaia 43, 113

Maslow: 'needs and wants' 7
Metabolisation 8,9; of nature 46, 61, 111, 113–114, 128, 133, 138, 141–144, 148; industrial 44, 70, 111, 131
Mexico: and economy 14–15; and environmentalists 35
Montreal Convention 93
Montreal Protocol 30, 81

Natural gas 62–63; and Brazil 102–103; *see also* Energy
Natural systems 39, 43–47, 111–113, 130–131
Natural resource accounting 114–115
'Needs and wants': Maslow 7
New Economics Foundation (NEF) 54–57
Non-governmental organisations (NGOs) 7, 117; and Earth Summit 23, 117; and international policies 32
Nuclear power 97; and Brazil 103; *see also* Energy

Objectivism 145–146
Oil: and Brazil 102–103; and China 78; exporters 68; and OPEC 14, 76, 62, 63; *see also* Energy, Hydrocarbons
Organisation for Economic Cooperation and Development (OECD): and environmental models 155–156; and industry 70, 93; and sustainability indicators 54
Organisation of Petroleum Exporting Countries (OPEC): and climate change 24; *see also* Oil
Our Common Future Brundtland Commission report 18
Overconsumption 6–7

Participation: public involvement 32, 107–108, 117, see *also* Local

environmental action
Phenomenology 145–146
Policies: Brazilian energy 100–108;
    energy 91–108; European energy
    92–100; environmental
    management 31–38; international
    environmental 12–31; and
    sustainability targets 57–59
Politics: democracy and environment
    117–119; and global environmental
    problems 109–110, 114, 116–119,
    128–129, 135, 139, 140, 149
Pollution 82–90, 116, 149, 150, 153, 155,
    156; and abatement 98–100;
    description 144–148; and models
    155–156; *see also* CFCs,
    Contaminated land, Emissions,
    Greenhouse gases, Hazardous
    waste, Hydrocarbons, Toxic waste,
    Transport
Population: and Brazil 101, 107; and
    Earth Summit 20, 22; and emissions
    99, 149; and energy consumption 71
Poverty: and Earth Summit 21; and
    international economy 16–17,
    72–73; and powerlessness 118–119;
    and sustainable development 123;
    and waste disposal 123
Pressure-state-response (PSR) model
    155–156

Quality of life 119–123

Recovering consumption 2, 4, 8, 10, 71,
    82–90, 149–150, 153–156
Recycling 43–44, 82–83, 113, 115,
    129–130, 153, 155
Royal Commission on Environmental
    Pollution 153–154

Science: research 46–47; *see also*
    Uncertainty
Sewage 44, 125, 154
Sinks 3–4, 20–22, 40, 43–44, 46–47, 64,
    111, 113, 123–131, 135, 138–139,
    141–144, 148; and Amazon 9, 108;
    social functions of 129–132
Social practices and environment
    133–136, 144–148, 159–160; *see also*
    Lifestyle

Sociology: and consumption 4–6,
    110–111, 113–114, 131–136,
    144–150, 159–160; and
    environmental discourse 136–148;
    and environmental management
    133–141; and objectivism 145–146;
    and phenomenology 145–146; *see
    also* Behaviour
Standard of living 20, 121–123, 140, 149;
    and consumption classes 119–123;
    and income 72–74
Stockholm Conference on the Human
    Environment 12–13
Supply depot: environment as 134
Sustainability 2, 11, 91, 149, 158; and
    culture 9; indicators and objectives
    9, 49–59, 116–117; and institutions
    1; local 151; and welfare 10
Sustainable development 1–2, 47–49,
    115; and policies 18, 36–38, 39–40,
    57–58, 91, 100, 110, 115, 126–128,
    150; and Amazon 102, 106–108
Systems: natural 39, 43–47, 111–113,
    130–131; industrial 111–113, 131

Technology: 'clean' 22–23, 30, 86,
    99–100, 126; environmental impacts
    68–71, 116, 140, 149; and energy
    consumption 92–93, 99; and food
    production 148; and waste disposal
    154–155
Technology 'foresight' 5
Thermodynamics: and global
    environmental change 42–44, 130
Toxic waste 86–89, 140, 154, 155; *see
    also* Hazardous waste
Transport: and pollution 83–86, 116;
    and standards 53; *see also* Cars

United Nations Conference on
    Environment and Development
    (UNCED); and biodiversity 27–28;
    and climate change 21, 23–26; and
    developing countries 29–30, 24–26;
    and emissions 25, 123; and
    environmental management 8, 11,
    19–22, 24–38, 109–110; and finance
    28–31; and forest principles 26–27;
    and global environmental change

22; and hazardous waste 22; and non-governmental organisations 117, 23; and population 20, 22; run-up to 19–22; and sustainability indicators 52–54
Uncertainty: of knowledge 136–137, 140, 144

Voluntary Service Overseas (VSO) 158

Waste: disposal 82–83; incinerators 154–156; industrial 82; and landfill 82–83, 113, 129, 153; municipal 82; *see also* Hazardous waste, Pollution, Emissions
Ways of seeing Berger, John 150
Welfare: and consumption 2–3, 10,

149–150; and trade 19; *see also* Inequality
World Bank: and environmental policy 117–118; and global economy 16–19; and policy finance 29–31; and World Development Report 123; *see also* Global Environment Facility
World Commission on Environment and Development (Brundtland Commission) 18, 23, 39–40, 47, 59, 117
World Conservation Strategies 14, 117, 112–113
World Development Report 123
World Resources Institute 124, 129
World Wide Fund for Nature (WWF) 54–57